# SUBSTANCE

## &

# EVIDENCE

### DISCOVERING FAITH THROUGH CRISES

## DARIUS MCDANIEL

# Copyright Notice

# Dedication

This work is dedicated to everyone in the daily fight of faith. My hope and prayer is that through this book, God will grow your faith and you will have the proper weapons to know and understand that the fight of faith is a fixed fight. To my wife, family, and friends: This book is also dedicated to you for your unwavering support and love through every part of my faith-journey.

There has been so much that you have walked with me through, seen me overcome and am still overcoming. If it wasn't for my family, I would be on other paths not writing this book. Most importantly, I dedicate this book to God Almighty and the amazing revelation He has given me through the various tests and trials I've endured this far. Thank you, Father, for all you have taken me through and what you will pour into the lives of those venturing to read this book.

# Acknowledgments

- **To my wife**: Thank you for everything you have let the Lord reveal to you about our lives and family. Thank you for being a woman of prayer, wisdom, and encouragement. You are truly a gift from God who I am grateful for. I love you!

- **To my family**: Thank you for your love, encouragement, and support through every test and milestone in my life.

- **To my friends**: You are the best and I couldn't ask for better people to do life with. I love you and am grateful for your wise counsel.

- **To my mentors and coaches**: Thank you for seeing things in me that I didn't see or understand I could and would accomplish. Thank you for accepting the call to impart the knowledge and understanding you've obtained into the next generation.

- **To Pastor Patrice and Apostle Bryan Meadows**: Thank you for being our friends and spiritual covering. The example you both set encourages and builds our faith in so many ways. I love you both.

- **To My Publisher**: Thank you for helping make this book clear and concise. Thank you for your time and coaching to bring structure and guidance to the vision through words.

# Table of Contents

# Introduction

Today, we encounter distractions from various local to global news sources, and more than ever, from social media outlets. Our world is full of so-called experts of various subjects trying to bombard us with untested and unapplied information. We have information flowing into our lives via notifications attached to apps on our cellular devices and through many other mediums.

Advertisements between television shows and the sporting events we enjoy are laced with messages that seduce us into purchasing products. Or we hear the fear-tactics of drug makers who warn us about devastating diseases, trying to force us into purchasing the drugs they've created. Of course, these drugs have side effects that make us wonder why we would even consider taking them. We may even receive hundreds of emailed advertisements and promotions trying to get us to subscribe to services we may have used for a one-time purchase. They seduce us with discounts and timers, and we often fall for it.

Information is vital to everything we do, but unfortunately, we can all become trapped by misinformation or small parts of a story. At some point in life, we discover that the information we once believed to be true is maybe slightly incorrect or taken out of context.

We are given pieces of the puzzles, so we fail to test the information provided. We run with things that lack credibility in our attempts to seem smart, but this only reveals our ignorance and how much we don't know. It is human nature for us to want to know as much as possible to survive, but with this information comes limitations and hidden agendas.

We are misguided by statistics, and we fail to ask the question, "Where do these numbers come from, and are they valid?" Trust is placed in media and lack of understanding is ever-present. Our faith is challenged every day when we allow the horrific stories with the titles such as "Breaking News" or "Late Breaking" to desensitize us.

Millions place trust in political leaders for change, and all too often, they are met with lies. Consequently, when we base our lives on what we see and hear through the lens of the media, we often find ourselves trapped and going around in circles. This is how belief systems are created, and these belief systems are hard to break without the proper tools.

Not only are we bombarded with stories daily, but we are also inundated with information from the conversations we have with the people around us, mostly family, friends, acquaintances, and co-workers. Others filter information through their personal lenses, and then deliver this information to us. This is how we find ourselves believing things we took little to no time vetting.

In March 2020, our lives were forever changed with the news that an invisible virus called SARS-COV2, better known as Covid-19 had been declared a global pandemic. There was an outbreak happening that would change all of our lives. Having worked and studied in public health, I knew this was extremely serious.

In my training at Emory University, we studied preparedness and response; we explored models and learned of viruses that were epidemics in many nations outside of the U.S. I recall one of my professors emphasizing that we are not prepared for a pandemic level outbreak. This was what we saw unfolding before our eyes in 2020.

With this outbreak came multiple sources of misinformation that flooded the media airways. Scientific information from what experts knew about diseases like Coronavirus had multiple holes in it. New so-called epidemiological evidence on the spread and biological aspects of the virus came out daily, and this birthed more fear.

Our governmental agencies and leaders were misleading millions of people daily with information that had not withstood the test of time. They didn't know what to do, and it would have been great for us to hear them admit this more often. We just needed to know that we all were in this together. Just a little sense of hope is what people around the world were searching for.

Fear took over and faith seemed to be disregarded all around the world. Conspiracies ran wild through communities and caused many to lose their lives. One of the wildest conspiracies was the 5G Coronavirus theory. It really made headlines, and many believed it. I mean people absolutely believed that cell phones were the super spreaders of Covid-19. Hope as we know it became dark because millions were searching for something to believe in.

What we saw, heard, touched, tasted, and smelled were all impacted from this new level of fear produced from an invisible enemy. This enemy didn't care about who you were or where you were.

This new invisible enemy coined the slogan "Wear a mask," and it produced shutdown orders first of its kind. We knew little about what the proper mask protection was or if it could truly protect us. I've lived through blizzards and tornadoes that caused state of emergencies with a few days of school closing, but never imagined a full shutdown for months.

Our lifestyles, habits, and routines came under attack from every angle or were halted indefinitely. Unimagined and unheard-of pivots needed to be made on every front. Millions lost their sources of income, and they didn't know if they would be able to provide food and shelter for their loved ones.

Everything shut down except for essential workers and companies. This word "essential" had new definitions emerging daily and it became a well-known term. Working from home became the hot topic; this had been a pre-Covid concept, but now, it had suddenly become the only option for some.

The pandemic had me constantly wanting to learn the depths of the disease and the breadth of its reach, so that I could be informed. This would allow me to help my family and friends stay safe. Within months, we would hear and see that millions would have contracted the disease, and many would lose the fight of their lives to this virus. An unprecedented race was occurring to find treatments and vaccines to combat the virus with.

What we all witnessed unfolding was a crash of systems, and one of those systems in particular was healthcare. All other diseases took a backseat because of the strain and unpreparedness of our healthcare systems. There were massive shortages of proper safety protection all around the world.

There were bidding wars happening in the healthcare industry to get ventilators and proper protection equipment. We came to learn how globally connected we are and how much we really depended on other nations to produce products of the utmost importance. I mean life or death determining products.

> *"Do not be anxious about anything, but in every situation, by prayer and petition, with thanksgiving, present your requests to God. And the peace of God, which transcends all understanding, will guard your hearts and your minds in Christ Jesus."*
>
> *Philippians 4:6-7 (NIV)*

Throughout 2020, we felt the anxiety and pain in many areas of our lives. Many who seemed to have prayer lives pre-Covid lost their faith, while others gained a new level of prayer. Not contracting this deadly disease was our main concern. We were worried about things beyond our control; this took hold of our hearts and minds. The feeling of dark days with no light consumed us with only COVID being heard and showcased all around.

Even though the depiction through the lens of the media sources was doom and gloom, millions of people around the world had hope that this horrific pandemic would pass, and we knew who was in control. Hope still existed, and there was proof that this invisible enemy wouldn't win.

But this invisible enemy wasn't the only pandemic plaguing our communities. The all-so-familiar racial divide was front stage again through the killing of unarmed black men at the hands of the police. The killing of George Floyd brought the Black community to its wits' end after spending so many years tolerating the system of oppression. Many felt unheard, so millions peacefully protested globally, while others looted.

For many of us, this was a constant occurrence. Questions arose regarding the end of the racial divide. The fear of being shot by an ignorant person became more of a reality every time we saw blue and red lights. Many still believe that individual people need to be blamed, but it is the systems that needed complete overhauls.

Pain and fury arose in many communities causing a widespread hatred from others who didn't understand or try to understand. We were fighting a battle on all fronts.

Now, the question is, would our faith really grow and would unsupported belief systems within our nation change? Or was this just another highlight in an evil cycle that would eventually show up again? Would our faith have grown enough to survive the next heart-breaking news?

Within this book, we will explore the concept, the law, and the principle of faith. We will learn from many personal stories and biblical stories, and these stories will hopefully bring clarity and become useful to building our faith.

Since battles are won in our minds, we will come to understand how what we hear and focus on provides access to important areas, and if not protected, these access points can have devastating impacts on our minds. Overall, our mission within this book is simply to paint a picture that would allow us to strengthen our understanding of faith. This is so we will better understand that endurance and perseverance are needed regardless of what troubling seasons we find ourselves in. Our goal for this book is to plant or water seeds that the Lord will use to push you to the next level on your faith-journey. We pray that through this book, God gets all the glory, and all other voices of evil intent are bound, in the name of Jesus.

# Chapter 1

## (You are Not Alone)

In 2008, I stood in a place where I believed others had my future in their hands. Prior to this moment, I was afraid that all I'd dreamed of doing and accomplishing were about to be snatched away. I was about to make a decision that would absolutely change everything in my life. I questioned everything and gave my all to the investigators searching for evidence that the judge could use for a conviction. I knew I was wrong, and I was willing to face the consequences. But somehow, I still seemed to be able to focus, even though I had a massive decision lurking over my head that had to be made. Only my family and close friends of the family knew the details, and some of them were extremely worried about this upcoming moment.

One individual seemed not to worry at all. I wondered how he could stay calm and not be angry or disappointed. He had worked his whole life, and now this issue was hitting his family as well. He'd sacrificed so much, and his encouragement confused me. I had known about biblical characters who'd exhibited strong faith, but never thought I would see it exemplified from someone so close to me. There was something within this man that I wanted to know more about. I never understood this place he operated in until I started having family and friends go through grief and other challenging moments with me. I would ask myself if we'd really survive after these difficult seasons with our minds intact.

For years, I thought and believed that the people around me simply didn't go through anything and would never understand what I'd encountered. What was I truly witnessing and experiencing that couldn't be explained until years later?

Daily, we see and hear motivational speakers, musicians, and preachers try to bring hope to our situations by saying that the seasons we were in would pass with us coming out stronger. But, in those unknowing and tumultuous seasons, are we hearing them and holding on to the faith they seem to have?

I don't believe I heard anything except for the music that I listened to daily. I was at my lowest point, trying to figure out how to avoid the decision I had to make. I spent quite a bit of time asking God if I could just go back in time to make a better choice.

At this juncture of my life, I still had this level of focus; this possibly stems from me being an athlete preparing for collegiate athletics. I was going on recruitment visits for football while competing in my high school's final track and field season. Hope of finishing with multiple scholarships for football and track helped me to remain focused.

Internally, my hope in the next level had become desolate, but externally, I tried hard to just put on a show and run my best. By this, I mean run until I had an injury that should have taken me out, but it didn't. I was a hurdler and I'd experienced a blow to an area that I didn't know was crucial for my success.

During one of the final track-meets of the regular season, my arch cracked. At the time, the Roosevelt Invitational Track Meet was where some of the best runners showcased their talents in the Midwest region. I had managed not only to injure myself in the semifinals, but also run one of the top eight times to make it to the finals. This was painful, but somehow, I ran and ran through the pain. A little of it was also pride because my brother who was a rising track star in the nation also made it to the finals in the 300-meter hurdles.

I remember the race like it was yesterday. I had made up in my mind that my brother would not beat me here. He didn't beat me that time, but he would eventually do so years later in college. I was excited to see his growth.

After that race, I went to see different doctors, and this is when I learned that my season was over. After hearing this news, I felt like I was losing everything around me. This came a month or so before the decision of my life was to be made.

Thoughts of heading to the military suddenly began to inundate my mind, and those thoughts seemed to be promising. The military was a place I know would work no matter what the judge's decision was. The idea of going to college to run track had now taken the back seat. I tried to take control of my life, but I felt helpless.

The fear of not knowing what was next took a hold of me, but there were some scriptures that I could recall such as:

> *"Trust in the Lord with all thine heart; and lean not unto thine own understanding. In all thy ways acknowledge him, and he shall direct thy paths."*
>
> *Proverbs 3:5-6 (KJV)*

This brought me some level of peace. I had asked for forgiveness and believed to an extent that it was now in the Master's hands.

I tried to keep reminding myself of something my grandmother would often say, and that is, "Everything will work out for your good." Of course, this is a paraphrased version of Romans 8:28.

> *"And we know that all things work together for good to them that love God, to them who are the called according to his purpose."*
>
> *Romans 8:28 (KJV)*

Looking back at it now, I can say that everything would truly work out, but it did not seem that way when I was going through the storm.

In the book of Daniel, we read about three young men who found themselves facing a judgment of epic proportions. Primarily, chapter three gives us the story of Shadrach, Meshach, and Abednego, along with the fiery furnace judgment given to them by King Nebuchadnezzar.

The king had created a statue of himself and ordered all the nations to bow to and worship it.

> *"Whoever does not fall down and worship will immediately be thrown into a blazing furnace."*
>
> *Daniel 3:6 (NIV)*

This story resonated with me and gave me some hope; it was a familiar story that I'd remembered from Sunday school. Shadrach, Meshach, and Abednego didn't know that they would become powerful examples of faith in the midst of horrific circumstances. Could you imagine ever being thrown into fire? NO, NO and NO! Of course not! Nevertheless, these young men did not bow down.

In verses 19 through 22, we read that they had made the King so angry that he ordered the furnace that they were about to be thrown into to be made seven times hotter than it normally was. He also ordered some of his strongest men to tie them up and throw them into the fire.

This trust in God that Shadrach, Meshach, and Abednego stood on wasn't just for them. With the punishment of death, they would eventually discover that they were not alone and were being used to change the heart of the king.

The decision from my trial was in. The only thing I heard was, "Five years of probation and restitution for what was taken." That's when I fell to my knees and cried. My charges had been dropped from a felony offense to a misdemeanor. It seemed unreal because my attorney told me to embrace for the worst, but inside, I didn't truly believe him. I recall my attorney clear as day saying that I would be facing five years in prison and a felony charge for what would be known today as a white-collar crime. I was grateful and felt the mercy of God. My inability to truly believe what the attorney told me was something I couldn't explain.

The weight I felt in the courtroom trying to lord itself over my life was lifted. In that moment, I knew that there was a God because all I could do was trust that no matter what happened, I would survive. From that day forward, I was convinced that there was a larger plan for me, and nothing would stop me from believing God with everything and in everything. I was in the fire, but just like the Hebrew boys, God had been there with me.

I was almost convinced that I was going to be another number; I thought I would become a part of the ever-growing Black male incarceration statistics. Yes, I had made a mistake that should have left me with a felony conviction, but it didn't. What I learned was that something was working within me to bring forth the development of a mindset that we will explore in later chapters.

When my college friends faced trying times, I would always have encouraging words that sprung up from my hurt, shame, and pain. Years later, I would come to understand what was at work in me, and I started a journey of learning more about faith beyond just going to church.

I moved from Ohio to Alabama with an appreciation of the second chance I'd been given. I made up my mind that I wasn't going to waste this opportunity. A new world of learning experiences opened. My emotional, social, and relational intelligence would begin to grow.

Making the decision to attend a historically Black university became one of the best experiences in my life. It set up an unmovable framework that stood atop a solid foundation. The friendships and mentorships developed during this journey would set up lifelong relationships and help me learn more about myself.

In November 2008, during my first semester of college, news that Barack Obama had been elected as the 44th president flooded the airwaves. This news was historical. Hearing and experiencing this as a 19-year-old Black man on the campus of a Black university built for the advancement of people of color was indescribable. At that time, it felt as though everything that Blacks had fought for hadn't been in vain, and change was happening in our nation.

To millions of African Americans, this was a joyous occasion and a historical milestone, but it was also a sad one for many. Millions died and fought to see days like the ones I was living in. I have spoken to countless older men and women, and never did they think they would live to see an African American hold what is thought to be the highest office in the land.

President Obama had run on a platform of hope in a time during one of the most serious financial crises since the Great Depression, second to the COVID-19 recession. He found himself inheriting an economic meltdown in the most powerful country in the world, and this was something he had to fix. A Black Man. He faced hell from day one, but he persevered.

Reflecting on 2008, I learned that no matter what you have been or are currently going through, you are not alone. There are countless examples of men and women within the Bible who'd gone through things that we today would have thrown in the towel over. One thing that is critical to growth and overcoming fear through faith is that you must endure the tests and trials.

In Job 1:13-22, we are presented with a man named Job. He had lost almost everything! He's suffered through the death of his children to listening to his friends accuse him of wrongdoing. He lost sons and daughters, but he kept his trust in God. For his faithfulness during suffering, he was given much more than he had initially possessed.

There is power in knowing that you are not alone in the fight. In the coming chapters, we will explore the concept of faith, and we will be encouraged, understanding that the race isn't over. It's not a sprint but truly a marathon. Hurdles will be in our lanes that we have to go

over or straight through, but never around.
There is wisdom in endurance.

## Chapter 2

### (I Don't Know)

In August 2008, I went on to college to run track and major in mathematics while also having a probation officer who, at first, believed I wouldn't make it. Throughout college, I was tested with various temptations that tried to creep in to derail me from chasing my purpose and seeking understanding. I kept the belief that there was a larger plan at work in my life.

But there was something about the discipline from track and field that didn't just prove that physical fitness and training were important, but it revealed that the mind was the crucial piece to everything. Pushing past pain in the body isn't easy, but if you can push past it in your mind, everything else falls in line. Our high school track team had a slogan, which was *"Pain is a state of mind."* This slogan was on the back of our uniforms. This was basically ingrained in us. My coaches taught and drilled this concept in us from high school to college, each one in different ways. These men and women were crucial in helping me to learn to lean on them and others for what I did not know. They built upon the foundation my parents and grandparents provided at home.

Throughout college, I thought I knew a little something, but at the end of the day, I came to the realization that I didn't know anything. How to succeed in this new environment was something I needed help with. I remember my first year encountering a man who was a no-nonsense kind of guy. He was a part of a generation that had seen and been through so much, from Jim Crow to various assassinations and more. He had developed a drive to help young men and women to go pro in almost every sport or in other professional areas.

My first encounter with him was when he asked us new freshmen how many of us could do 100 push-ups straight. I stated, "*I can.*" I thought I knew how to do push-ups and went fast through them, and at the end, he said, "Hold it! Those are not push-ups." I looked like a fool because I didn't know how to do what seemed to be the simplest workout of them all. That day started my relationship with the statement, "I don't know, but God does."

I learned that God uses people to build us and fill in areas of our lives with information to help us know a little something. These people helped develop my knowledge in areas where I was ignorant.

Coach Lee became one of the most impactful men in my life. Not just in the physical aspect of discipline, but most importantly, in correcting me and providing wisdom for life. He was our strength and conditioning coach, but beyond just track. He saw things in me I never knew were in me. For one, he saw that I was a leader who needed development. He gave me the first leadership book in my library. This book was a game changer and brought clarity to things that were in the infancy stage within me. The book was known as "*The 21 Irrefutable Laws of Leadership*" by John Maxwell.

This book became the point in which I started to build on as a leader. One of the laws that resonated with me was "*The Law of Process.*" Here he states:

*"Although it's true that some people are born with greater natural gifts than others, the ability to lead is really a collection of skills, nearly all of which can be learned and improved. But that process doesn't happen overnight."*

It was without doubt that Coach Lee and other mentors in my life knew this principle in some form. Within this law, he gives four phases of leadership growth that I believed Coach Lee wanted me to know as I grew:

1. *I don't know what I don't know. ("As long as a person doesn't know what he doesn't know, he isn't going to grow.")*
2. *I know what I don't know. (Benjamin Disraeli, former British prime minister, wisely commented, "To be conscious that you are ignorant of the facts is a great step to knowledge.")*
3. *I know what I don't know. ("What is your plan for personal growth?")*

4. *I simply go because of what I know.
   ("When you recognize your lack of skill
   and begin the daily discipline of
   personal growth, exciting things start to
   happen.")*

I spent countless hours in his office learning and hearing stories about his life. These moments taught me how to listen and talk with very wise individuals. I came to value and respect the knowledge and understanding that had obviously come from a long life of experience and endurance.

There were only a few times I saw this man really laugh and that was when he called my name and said, *"Chip, peanut butter and jelly is the best thang on earth."* There were a handful of my teammates in the room, and we all laughed.

For years, through multiple internships, track meets, workouts, and other disappointments, he would ask me what I'd learned from those experiences and what areas I needed to improve in. Moments like these with Coach Lee and many other individuals like him helped provide insight into what endurance and perseverance meant, even through my ignorance. They knew things I didn't know, and I became comfortable knowing that one day, I would learn what they knew. I would someday understand that it was all a process.

Furthermore, I began to realize that God has planted things we need within people, and if we believe we already know something, we stagnate ourselves from wisdom and revelation. Consequently, we could find ourselves in a place constantly dealing with the same tests and trials that keep us in bondage. It can become a cycle of foolishness that is hard to break.

Let's glimpse into the Coronavirus pandemic. While writing this book, some vaccines have come to the market in record-breaking time, and this process is much different than the way we have known vaccines to come about. This new medical discovery has brought hope to people around the world. By fear or faith, millions are deciding to take these new vaccines with hopes of protecting themselves from this invisible enemy.

These are uncharted waters of development and innovation. There are uncertainties regarding whether or not these vaccines will be able to fight against new variants of the disease that are popping up around the world. These new Coronavirus messenger-RNA (also known as MRNA) vaccines are being used to fight and provide protection by triggering our immune systems, alerting it that there is an unknown enemy in the body.

Previously, well-known vaccines took years (not months) to be developed and had within them either a weakened virus or an inactivated virus to trigger an immune response. This discovery of using MRNA aims to teach your body how to make the necessary protein needed to fight COVID-19 on its own without introducing the body to the virus of some sort.

For many, there is not much hesitation to get this vaccine, but for others, there is a hesitancy to take the vaccine because it is still new, and this is understandable. This is especially true for African Americans because of the history of medical misconduct and unethical experiments on Blacks throughout the United States. A vaccine that has come to market can be questioned, and rightfully so, considering the history, other inequities, and disparities in healthcare that are still present to this day.

Though we hear and see-through numerous media outlets that these vaccines are new for Coronavirus, the research surrounding viruses is not new to the world of infectious diseases. In cancer research, this technological advancement is being used to teach the body how to create an immune response to target specific cancer cells. MRNA vaccine development has been studied on well-known epidemics such as Ebola, Zika and Influenza (Flu).

With anything new, processes/protocols have changed or are being developed and still have levels of uncertainty. In science, we try to use the best technology and relevant data for analyses to eliminate much of the "I don't know" factor, but uncertainty exists and can never go away.

The same thing is true for our lives. We don't know what tomorrow will bring or what the storm will teach us, but we do know this—it will teach us something and there will still be a tomorrow.

> *"Do not boast about tomorrow, for you do not know what a day may bring."*
> *Proverbs 27:1 (NIV)*

> *"Therefore do not worry about tomorrow, for tomorrow will worry about itself. Each day has enough trouble of its own."*
> *Matthew 6:34 (NIV)*

Paul wrote this while in prison:

> *"For to me, to live is Christ and to die is gain. If I am to go on living in the body,*

23

*this will mean fruitful labor for me. Yet what shall I choose? I do not know! I am torn between the two: I desire to depart and be with Christ, which is better by far; but it is more necessary for you that I remain in the body."*

*Philippians 1:21-24 (NIV)*

We don't know when the Coronavirus pandemic will end, but it will. Only God knows when it will end. It is important for us to realize that our work here isn't finished, even though plagues and disasters are rising up all around.

*"We are pressed on every side by troubles, but we are not crushed. We are perplexed, but not driven to despair. We are hunted down, but never abandoned by God. We get knocked down, but we are not destroyed."*

*2 Corinthians 4:8-9 (NLT)*

In future chapters, we will venture into the realm of uncertainty and how it is okay to say, "I don't know." That is, with the understanding that God knows everything and once we truly trust that His plans will be used to build our faith. In other words, we no longer need to worry or fear the decisions being made by men on our behalves.

## Chapter 3
# (Impostor, I am NOT)

There are many different belief systems in the world, and some of these systems can have detrimental effects on the way we see ourselves. These constructs place constraints on our focus and are used to make us believe that we don't belong.

What we hear from others around us can cause us to feel like we're not supposed to be here. But the true question is why don't we belong here?

Everyday, we are bombarded with data through two of our five senses. What we hear with our ears and see with our eyes. These two senses are the most important avenues in which data flows into our brains. Our minds are flooded by the millions of neurons at work that process information we are aware of (consciously) or unaware of (subconsciously). What we think isn't bothering or affecting us may be absolutely impacting us subconsciously.

There is a coined phrase that millions are grappling with; this phrase can either strengthen us or have us believing that we are inadequate and have nothing to contribute. This is better known as the Imposter Syndrome. Within this chapter, we will peel back this belief that has detrimental effects on our purpose, and if we don't confront it, we will have more generations struggling with their identities because of a lie.

In 2013, I entered graduate school for my Master's degree at Emory University. I had become the first in my family to make it that far. I could feel the weight of that burden, but I also had an unmatched level of excitement. I had come to a new city with around $1500 and I felt these funds would only last a while because of all the living expenses that had accrued just from the move. I had no job, and that was at the forefront of my mind.

I made friends from all different parts of the world. I soon started to admire and love the diversity of cultures within public health, but for the first time, I found myself as one of a handful of Black men in the school of public health. I was the only one pursuing a Masters in Biostatistics and Bioinformatics.

I made up in my mind that I would succeed in my fields, but this is when the challenges in my mind began to surface. For years prior to graduate school, I would hear a phrase that I didn't really understand coming from others who had gone through graduate school or were currently in graduate school. Their depiction of this thing was either dark or encouraging.

I started feeling out of place halfway through the semester when the time came for me to start studying for a particular midterm exam. I was doing very well understanding the material, but then came the test. I walked in focused like I was one of the runners at a track meet with all eyes on me. I took a glance at everyone in the room and almost everyone was of Asian descent.

For some reason, I felt as though I was in a competition again. At the same time, the $1500 I came to grad school with had depleted. A week prior to the exam I started a statistics' grad role making $15/hour, and I worked for 10-20 hours a week. This was basically enough to pay rent and splurge on a diet of Ramen noodles peppered with frozen vegetables. I knew how to survive having gone to an HBCU, but living like that had become challenging. I could feel the demands and pressure of everything resting on my shoulders.

During this test, I tried to ignore all my surroundings and circumstances, but I couldn't. I ended up failing that test. It was the first time I'd ever seen a score that was less than 70. I mean, it was a 19 out of 100. I believed I studied my rear end off, but it was not enough. I wanted to quit; I wanted to shout, "This is ridiculous! Who do I think I'm fooling?!" There was a flood of negative thoughts now starting to formulate in my mind.

Honestly, alcohol was becoming somewhat of a friend to me; it would help me to subdue the thoughts. Fear was creeping in. I started to lose focus. I didn't reveal what I was going through to anyone, and when asked how everything was going from mentors and family, I would lie and say, "Everything is going good."

From that day forward and just through that one failed test (in one out of four classes), a seed had been planted causing me to believe that I didn't belong there. Suddenly, I started revisiting the idea of joining the military, but this time, my drug of choice would be the Navy. I got real close to signing the papers.

Meanwhile, my five years of probation were coming to an end that upcoming December. I was becoming free from one thing while being bound by another. I was in bondage to the fear of failure, and there was no end in sight. I had proved to my probation officer that I could change my life for the better, but the limits placed on me were like shackles made of paper. In my mind, limiting thoughts began to swarm in.

Eventually, I failed that class and I started exploring other options that would utilize my mathematical and computational skills. I took the following semester off to work and explore other avenues.

What was this dilemma that millions faced when in environments that they are truly qualified for, that would make them feel completely out of place? It is called the Imposter Syndrome. What is *"Imposter's Syndrome"?* Impostor syndrome (IS) refers to an internal experience of believing that you are not as competent as others perceive you to be. Simplified, it is the experience of feeling like a phony, and believing that, at any moment, you will be found to be a fraud and it would be revealed to the people around you that you don't belong where you are. They would all discover that you only got there through some stroke of luck.

In an article titled *"How One Can Thrive Despite Experiencing Imposter Syndrome,"* Dr. Leilani Carver-Madalon, an associate professor of strategic communication and leadership defined Impostor Syndrome as the experience of someone who *"feels like a fraud, intellectually and/or professionally. People who are experiencing Imposter Syndrome feel like they are not good enough, like they don't belong and/or that they are a fraud, and it is only a matter of time before they will be found out."*

This terminology was invented in 1978 by two psychologists: Pauline Rose Clance and Suzanne Imes. They described Imposter Syndrome as an *"internal experience of intellectual phoniness in people who believe that they are not intelligent, capable or creative despite evidence of high achievement."* Their work hypothesized *"that the phenomenon only affected women and argued that sexist socialization messages encouraged men to externalize their failures and internalize successes while encouraging women to do the opposite."* After much more research into this, researchers have found that impostor feelings are not limited to women, with various studies now showing it to be associated with racial discrimination and impacting people of color at alarming rates.

In a paper entitled *"The Imposter Phenomenon Among Black Doctoral and Postdoctoral Scholars In STEM,"* Dr. Devasmita's team did extensive research into this belief on undergraduates and graduates. The objective was to study the effects of Imposter Syndrome on doctoral level Blacks. They conducted multiple studies on this and how it affected all genders, professions and people of color. One of which found that *"both racial identity and race-based discrimination increases impostor phenomenon"* (D. L. Bernard et al., 2018).

I believed this research because of how I felt being one of the only Black men in the room. I knew that I would be facing a series of statistics that predicted my failure, and it was my job to change those statistics, but I didn't understand the weight of my assignment until I met those feelings face to face.

During the break of grad studies, I took extra work, helping on multiple infectious disease projects. In February of 2014, one of the primary investigators asked me if I would like to go to South Africa to work on some projects. At that time, I was open to anything, so I agreed. I had never been out the country, and to be honest, I didn't really believe I would ever travel outside of the United States' borders.

A few months later, I started receiving emails reminding me to book my flight and other accommodations. Little did I know, this experience would change my life forever and be used to prove to me that I belonged right where God had placed me. This would allow my confessions and mindset to evolve.

At the end of May 2014, I was on a twenty-three-hour flight from Atlanta, Georgia to Johannesburg, South Africa with a layover in Dakar, Senegal. This flight by itself was amazing. From the food to the different cultures represented on this South African Airways flight were all eye-opening.

There, I developed friendships with some amazing people. I found a passion for the food and culture. My perspective on life was changing just by me seeing people of color in power and striving for more on a continent that the media tries to depict as impoverished and inferior.

While there, I started to learn in-depth about their history and culture. Similar to the Blacks in the United States, they had been through so much as a people. Listening to their views on Apartheid and their honor for the well-known and much-loved Nelson Mandela was mind-blowing. There, I had a chance to visit the Apartheid Museum, and oh did that experience bring so many tears to my eyes! I can recall walking into one part of an exhibit and seeing nooses hanging from the ceiling. It was painful to walk through and especially see people there not really understanding this.

You could still see the hardships and the division along with its devastating impacts. Just eating a meal at a nice restaurant right across the street and seeing a shanty town was humbling. To many people, seeing a young Black man working with doctors was amazing, but for me, meeting them was the experience that changed my mind; it helped me to see that I did belong and I truly had something to contribute.

The experience was indescribable. I had experienced southern hospitality in America, but it wasn't close to the love and hospitality I experienced in South Africa. It was so euphoric that I did not want to leave at all. I'm serious. I wanted to give up everything back in America and convince my family to move there. My family and some friends thought I was crazy, but there was a peace of mind there that could only be experienced and not spoken about.

During that time, I began reading the latest book release by Bishop T.D. Jakes called "Instinct." He was describing one of his life-changing experiences in South Africa while on a safari. He describes it as a *"truly life-transforming event."* This book, which had been inspired in and by South Africa, was being read by me in South Africa, and it was transformational in my life. This legendary work of art became one of the most influential, prophetic, and encouraging things I had ever read. While reading it, I was convinced he was speaking directly to me.

He made the statement:

*"If you have ever felt misaligned, this book is for you. If you have lost the rhythm, the passion, or the thrill of living in alignment that you once glimpsed, then keep reading."*

A few paragraphs later, he talked about his life saying, *"The only reason I moved beyond the many potholes and pit stops I encountered is because of an instinctive allure pulling me toward something up ahead on the road that I had to find! I refused to stop and settle for less than the explosive exploration of what God had placed within me."*

These statements encouraged me because I was feeling misaligned and lost. His words also reminded me that there were somethings I went to graduate school to find and learn, and if I didn't move forward, I would be settling for less than what God wanted for me.

All of this was just in chapter one! In chapter seven, he stated, *"Scripture tells us that deep calls out to deep, and I'm convinced that those people, places, and perspectives that resonate with us often do so because of a shared, kindred quality. When something you encounter resonates with you, pay attention. Become a student of your deepest passions and most persistent curiosities. Notice the people you admire and feel drawn to emulate. We instinctively recognize members of our own tribe, no matter how different they may look!"*

I started to remember that I was given mentors who had been in similar situations and recalled the experiences they'd shared. They were pioneers who I admired and loved learning from. These men and women invested time to pour into me and others aspiring to find their purposes. They saw that I was no imposter. Lastly, he quoted his friend Joyce Meyers, who said, *"Feel the fear and do it anyway!"* This propelled me to make the decision to stay in graduate school, but now with new clarity. With a newfound focus and vision, I declared that nothing or no one would stand in my way. I came to grips that failing was a part of life, and it was designed to teach me something.

In the fall of 2014, I took every class with the mindset that this wasn't for me, it is for all those before me who fought to give me a chance and for those in the next generation destined to build something great. One year later, I would go on to graduate with my Masters in public health.

I had to focus on not just being labeled as a statistician, but more. I took on the battle of dismantling fears and the systems that had taken out so many brilliant people because they believed they were a fraud.

The time will come when we will all face the thoughts that we are not enough, or we will never go further than where we've been. It's these voices that aim to attack our purpose and kill our dreams.

You do belong and you were created to be more than a conqueror so don't let anything come between that wisdom.

### An *IMPOSTER YOU ARE NOT!*

### Say this with me BOLDLY and LOUD: I AM NOT AN IMPOSTER!

You are only who God said you are.

## Chapter 4

# (Is Simply Believing Enough?)

Is believing in something the same as having faith in it? Are there differences in the concepts of faith and belief, or are they the same? Is it enough to simply believe that one day, I'll have a nice car and a beautiful house? We believe that we will have electricity and running water in our homes, but how?

Countries and people groups have risen and fallen on numerous beliefs. Empires were destroyed because of belief systems. Ideologies throughout history have given way to how we live today. If we never believed somethings, would we be living or existing?

There are many mindsets in the world, some of which have birthed amazing inventions, but on the other hand, have created inherently systemic belief structures. These systems have killed and destroyed millions of families and caused some groups and languages to become extinct or almost nonexistent.

The belief that one people group is superior to all others has created deep-rooted divisions that are seen in health and wealth disparities. It is also seen through hate crimes and killings via mass shootings. Strong men and women standing for equality and justice have been slain in front of millions.

The belief that an unarmed black man is so dangerous that lethal force must be used to subdue him is prevalent now more than ever, and we can see this through the many police shootings we've witnessed on the news or through social media.

Slavery was created from the notion that the gods created all other people groups inferior to just one other race. The belief that Blacks were just three-fifths human was published in the founding documents of America. Segregation laws were made and the slogan "separate but equal" started being propagated.

America was founded under the idea of "freedom for all", but this idea was not at all true. Owning slaves was the norm; free (forced) labor built the foundation of the country we've come to call home. Millions placed their trust in the concept of White supremacy, while others hoped that this lie would one day be dismantled and uprooted.

Scientists and researchers believed that Blacks could take more pain than their White counterparts, and consequently, they performed unethical experiments on Black bodies without consent or anesthesia. These set beliefs and practices created via eugenics caused Americans to believe some social groups are biologically "better" than others, and that scientific "reality" should drive social policies and technological interventions.

In eugenic thinking, the well-being of these superior people should be promoted: viewed as "positive" eugenics, and dates back to the English statistician Francis Galton, who coined the term "hereditarily endowed with noble qualities" in 1883 and encouraged the breeding of people.

Everything was created by just a thought, but it was the belief that they could accomplish it that gave way to people wanting to act on it. Whatever you think on can create beliefs that are empowering or oppressive. They can help build or be used to destroy and kill innocent children, women, and men.

We can believe something and it doesn't affect our lives, but when it does affect us or others, the effects can be either great or devastating. I believe that oceans exist, but I don't live my life differently because of this belief. However, I do enjoy going to the beach for relaxation and I love to explore the amazing marine life found in the ocean.

Just because I believe something doesn't make me place trust in it. I believe money answers all things, but if I have none, it's because I'm missing some other principles.

What I have come to learn is that beliefs and faith are not the same. I believe planes can get me from one place to the other faster than cars or trains, but if I'm afraid to board the plane, I then reveal that I have no faith in this mode of travel.

I've heard people say that they believe there is a God and that they believe in Him my entire life. I've also heard people say that there is no God and that the other antithetical ideologies are true. This has led me to the realization that these two concepts are different, meaning they oppose each other. The confusion that exists between these essential terms can create crises that seem insurmountable in our lives, especially when faith is needed the most. We can find ourselves searching for an understanding of what faith is and how bringing out an army of beliefs doesn't work.

We find out that our beliefs, whether they are strong, deep, broad, educated, magical or divine, do not help at all in raging storms. I believe in God, but I now know that I had no true trust in Him, and this could be seen in multiple situations that I'd found myself in.

We believe and say that He will make a way out of no way, but do we trust that He will? Do we trust that all things are working together for our good and for the good of them who love the Lord? I can believe that things are working for my good; that is until it seems they aren't, and this can and has derailed my faith. This always resulted in me attempting to take matters into my own hands, trying to fix whatever issues I'm presented with. I've relied on quick fixes to make me feel better as many others have. Going out and doing things opposite of what He told us to do is not trust.

We choose what we want to believe God for, but don't show that we trust Him with it. Money is a good example. We believe Him for money in the mail, but don't trust Him with giving us the wisdom needed to steward what He has already given us. Therefore, belief is simply acceptance of something in our minds, but it really doesn't affect the things in our lives. You can say you believe, but that alone never changes situations. Many of our beliefs are limited in depth, range, and scope, and are rooted in our culture and upbringing.

Sometimes, our most closely held beliefs are in direct conflict with everything else we know to be true.

Faith is birthed when a belief partners with understanding, hearing and the confidence built through action. It is trusting in God no matter what is thrown your way. Faith is a product of the spirit which pushes you beyond the circumstances, whereas belief is of the mind, and of course, the mind has limitations.

One of the most quoted scriptures on faith is Hebrews 11:1:

> *"Now, faith is the substance of things hope for, the evidence of things not seen."*

For years, I heard messages taught in different ways about faith, and some of those messages made sense while others confused me. I believed these teachers of the gospel had deep revelation of some sort. I studied up on faith and learned more about it; this helped me to piece together some surface-level views, but I was void of understanding regarding the topic.

It wasn't until I started listening to Dr. Myles Munroe, Dr. Tony Evans, Dr. Fredrick K.C. Price, and Bishop T.D. Jakes that I began to get a more in-depth grasp on the subject at hand. These men felt like gifts sent just to help me to piece together the puzzle of faith. I'd forgotten that one of these men helped the man I mentioned in chapter one to stay calm and unmoved in that storm. My father.

First, let us explore the context in which this powerful scripture was written to better understand its application. Hebrews is said to be one of the most difficult books to interpret, second only to Revelations. This book's author is unknown. It is debated and speculated that the writer could be Paul, Timothy, Luke, Apollos, and many others.

It is very interesting that this book of the Bible, which has the most prolific definition of faith at its core, has no clear author. Everywhere faith is taught in the Bible has an author we can ascribe the book to.

When we study Hebrews 11:1, it may be helpful to try and understand that the book of Hebrews is a book that is a connecting link between the Old and New Testaments. The book of Hebrews displays what faith does, with Hebrews 11:4 being known as "Faith's Hall of Fame." Scriptural references of faith in this chapter connect the actions of some people to their belief systems. These stories are used to depict true examples of how faith responds to varying trials and tests. These individuals provide proof that through various circumstances, we must maintain confidence in His promises and meditate on what He has said or saying.

Within Faith's Hall of Fame, we get a glimpse of what the faith that made men, women and people groups accomplish the impossible, even when they had to do it alone. The writer or writers of Hebrews provide us with the testimonies of individuals who had what we've come to know as crazy faith.

Could you imagine your mother, wife, sister, or friend coming to a point where she believes that she can have a child when she is over the age of 60 like Sarah? Would you have ever placed your child in a river, trusting that God would use him to free enslaved people like Moses' mother did? Would you believe that child would create ten fundamental principles that would someday become the foundations to every law in the world?

Theologian Thomas Aquinas paraphrased Hebrews 11:1 as: *"Faith is a settled disposition of the mind that allows the intellect to ascend to things that are not apparent."* True faith is not a statement of beliefs, but a state of being. Modern ideologies have been misguiding entire generations through a bunch of hollow philosophies that have no substance; they are just mere ideas and thoughts that amount to nothing truly. The education we've received or aspire to receive can confuse us or has confused us and made it difficult for us to know what we should believe versus what we should not believe. Many are aspiring to become educated fools led by blind philosophers who toy around with theories regarding how to live or how life was created.

Why don't we read the Bible? Is it possible that we think that we need the information in the book? Many believe that the Bible is useless until they are in trying times. "Outside of this situation, what can it do for me?" This is the standard line of reasoning that many Christians are submitted to. In other words, there is a war within us between our beliefs and the Word of God.

Many men and women have been given insight into the Word of God, and have used this insight to create books and powerful sermons. Their messages help us to get understanding and wisdom, not just mere knowledge that inflates. The fundamental question is: does

God have our trust for every area of our lives, even when we don't see it? Not just for our careers and families, but for EVERYTHING! The situations that appear to be dead ends don't matter or, better yet, are powerless when faith enters the picture. We often wonder why or how we've endured the hardships and trials that we've endured, and this question may never come with an answer that we can understand with our finite minds. Some questions are better left unanswered until God reveals the mysteries surrounding them.

In chapter three, we talked about how not knowing the answer to a mystery (in the context of faith) allows us to remain humble, grateful, and teachable. It is important to toss away the conflicting ideologies and unusable beliefs that come after our minds. Wherever there are cracks in our faith, fear is waiting to come and fill those hollow spaces.

## Chapter 5

# (This Thing Must Be Cultivated)

In Genesis 37, we are introduced to a young man by the name of Joseph. He is his father's favorite son. Joseph has many brothers who are jealous of him, and one day, he has a dream that reveals that his brothers would someday bow down to him. Rather than keeping his vision to himself, he shared his dreams with his brothers.

He was probably pretty humble when he'd had and shared the first dream, but the second dream was different. He'd dreamed of his entire family bowing to him, and it is during this space of time that we can see pride starting to surface. At this point, his brothers are furious, so they started devising a strategy to get rid of him. They eventually decided to sell him into slavery, instead of killing him.

Joseph became a slave in the house of a man named Potiphar. Potiphar was one of

Pharaoh's officers, and not just any officer, he was the captain of Pharaoh's guard. This means that Joseph had landed at the house of an important and highly regarded person. Instead of becoming bitter, he worked to grow his relationship in trusting God. He eventually found favor with Potiphar.

> *"Potiphar noticed this and realized that the Lord was with Joseph, giving him success in everything he did. This pleased Potiphar, so he soon made Joseph his personal attendant. He put him in charge of his entire household and everything he owned."*
>
> *Genesis 39:3-4 (NLT)*

This seemed to be the environment in which Joseph would be elevated towards the vision he'd revealed to his family. But no, Joseph had a new issue to deal within this atmosphere. Potiphar's wife started to have feelings for him and tried multiple times to have sex with him. He'd refused her advances each time she'd tried to seduce him, so she eventually elected to lie on him and accuse him of sexual assault.

Following this accusation, Potiphar had him thrown into prison.

Joseph could have been bitter and resentful, but instead, he decided to work on his relationship with God. He continued to trust in the Lord, and as a result of his faith, he found favor in this environment:

> *"But the Lord was with Joseph in the prison and showed him his faithful love. And the Lord made Joseph a favorite with the prison warden. Before long, the warden put Joseph in charge of all the other prisoners and over everything that happened in the prison. The warden had no more worries, because Joseph took care of everything. The Lord was with him and caused everything he did to succeed."*
>
> *Genesis 39:21-23 (NLT)*

Being in this new environment allowed him to meet a cupbearer and a baker who both worked for Pharaoh, but had somehow found themselves in prison as well. Both men had some crazy dreams that Joseph ended up interpreting for them with accuracy. The cupbearer eventually got out of prison and told Joseph that he would help him to get out.

Time went by and the cupbearer had forgotten about Joseph. But one day, Pharaoh had two dreams that disturbed him. He called upon his wisest men and the magicians close to him, and no one could interpret the dream. The cupbearer then remembered the man who'd helped him with his dream in prison and told Pharaoh about him. Joseph was called upon to interpret the dream. Before Pharaoh started to tell him the dream, Joseph shifted the credit from himself by mentioning that it's beyond his power to interpret the dreams, but that God would tell him what they meant. Joseph shifted the focus away from himself and gave God the glory. After this, Pharaoh told his dream to him. With God's help, Joseph interpreted the dream.

> *"So Pharaoh asked his officials, "Can we find anyone else like this man so obviously filled with the spirit of God?" Then Pharaoh said to Joseph, "Since*

> *God has revealed the meaning of the*
> *dreams to you, clearly no one else is as*
> *intelligent or wise as you are. You will*
> *be in charge of my court, and all my*
> *people will take orders from you. Only I,*
> *sitting on my throne, will have a rank*
> *higher than yours."*
>
> *Genesis 41: 38-40 (NLT)*

Joseph was placed as second in command, and what he'd said about Pharaoh's dreams came to pass. The dreams that Joseph had depicting his entire family bowing down to him would also start to play out.

Clearly, there is a lot to unpack from the life of Joseph. We could talk about his pride, him learning to keep the vision to himself, being sold into slavery, the coat of many colors and much more. But for this chapter, we will dive into the cultivation of Joseph's faith from the point of the two seeds or, better yet, dreams that had been planted in him. This planting birthed his gift of administration in which he used to build and cultivate others around him.

He could have allowed pride to convince him to keep those dreams to himself, or used his family drama and trauma as an excuse for him not cultivating his gift. He could have used his lack of training as an excuse as well. He could have waited for someone else to interpret the dream or affirm him whenever he interpreted the dream, but he didn't.

Even though he didn't realize this, but the cultivation and the understanding of his dreams would only come from the various tests and challenges he would face in his life. This would lead him to develop a relationship with God, and through that relationship, he would be used by God to bring revelation to God's people.

*"Everyone holds his fortune in his own hands, like a sculptor the raw material he will fashion into a figure. But it's the same with that type of artistic activity as with all others: We are merely born with the capability to do it. The skill to mold the material into what we want must be learned and attentively cultivated."*

*Johann WolfGang von GOETHE*

In nature, what makes a seed become a tree? Do all seeds grow to their full capacity or even grow at all? Do certain types of seeds only grow in certain climates and soil types? These are a few foundational questions that scientists had to answer if they were to understand how a seed could reach its full potential or become unfruitful.

Seeds have the capacity to become trees of different sizes, shapes, and colors. Some trees are very small, while others are extremely large. They can produce fruit or provide the nutrients or processes needed for the ecosystem around them to flourish.

There are over 60,000 different species of trees, according to Botanical Gardens Conservation International. Regardless of their size, these trees are home to millions of different types of insects and animals all around the world.

Varying aspects of a tree contribute to how much a tree can hold, store, and produce.

There are a couple of fundamental ingredients needed for a seed to become a tree of some sort. Three of the most important components for proper growth of a tree are climate, water, and dirt. First is the environment, climate, or region for growth. A tree's survival and production in a climate that is cold will be much different than one grown in a hotter atmosphere. Let's look at trees that survive some of the harshest conditions; that is the cold of winter.

There are various types of trees that can withstand some of the coldest climates. These trees have developed several ways to tolerate the freezing cold found in different regions of the world. The trees found here create a covering that serves to protect them; this covering is called a bark. The bark of a tree provides it with the insulation and protection needed to prevent cracking and freezing during the winter. These types of trees know when to drop their leaves or their needles. This process reduces the amount of water that can be lost. The trees which have needles are better at retaining water because of their small surface area and the waxy coating outside of them.

Lastly, trees that live in cold climates have a tolerance at a cellular level. The National Forest Foundation states the following about cell survival:

*"Trees begin to prepare for an oncoming winter in late summer as daylight hours decline, entering a dormant state and reaching their adapted tolerance by mid-winter. Through a combination of cellular changes that involve shrinkage, dehydration, and sugar concentration, the cells harden and become glasslike. This helps prevent freezing and damage to living cells."*

Some of these well-known trees are maple, oak, pine, and various apple trees. These trees produce either sweeteners, strong wood to build with or fruit for us to eat. If we were to plant seeds or move trees that are meant to be grown in warmer climates to colder ones, few may adapt and grow, but most would die. This shows us that many seeds never make it to tree formation because they are planted in environments that they weren't created for or environments that are not suitable for their growth. The place in which Joseph had grown up was necessary for a part of his development, but after he'd had the dreams, he had to be shifted. If he'd stayed in his home environment, his dreams would have died. Him being betrayed and sold off into slavery by his brothers was a pivotal point of his development. This event placed him in the right spaces for him to grow. It is essential for us to learn and understand that there are atmospheres and environments needed for the seeds planted within us to grow.

Secondly, along with the environment, water is essential for the growth of a seed. Too much water can cause trees in a colder climate to burst and die. And if there is flooding in a region, it can be fatal to a tree as well. In hotter climates, not having enough water can cause a shortage of the production of fruits or cause produce in general to become non-existent. If there is a drought in an area, that drought could become detrimental for the trees native to that area.

Water is vital to a tree's growth, production, and survival. Water helps trees develop the roots needed to hold the tree up; this allows the trees to be productive above ground and fulfill their purpose. The roots of a tree are an essential element used to transport nutrients from the soil to the tree. Depending on the type of tree, water on just the surface level is not enough. Deep watering is needed to promote the depths of root growth for trees; this helps them to become drought tolerant.

Finally, without dirt (soil), no seed can grow into a tree. The proper soil type is foundational to any seed's growth, both underground and above the surface. The soil is the storage place for water. It is the place where minerals and nutrients dissolve into the water to help foster seed growth and a productive tree life. The soil is also the place for roots to run deep or stay shallow.

There are numerous types of soil. In an article titled *"The Tree and The Soil"* by Elliot Menashe, the author states: *"Soils vary considerably in fertility, texture, color, depth, acidity, ability to hold water, and in many other ways, depending on:*

1) *the type of rocks from which the soils were formed.*
2) *the climate (hot or cold, wet or dry).*
3) *the trees, bushes, and other plants growing in the soils.*
4) *the animal and bird life of the areas.*
5) *whether the soils weathered in place from the bedrock or were moved to the places they now rest by ice (glaciation), water (streamflow), gravity (sliding), or wind.*
6) *slope of the land.*
7) *age, and other factors."*

In the book of Matthew, Jesus speaks through a story about a farmer and the importance of seeds being planted in the right soil:

> *"Then he told them many things in parables, saying: "A farmer went out to*

*sow his seed. As he was scattering the seed, some fell along the path, and the birds came and ate it up. Some fell on rocky places, where it did not have much soil. It sprang up quickly, because the soil was shallow. But when the sun came up, the plants were scorched, and they withered because they had no root. Other seed fell among thorns, which grew up and choked the plants. Still other seed fell on good soil, where it produced a crop—a hundred, sixty or thirty times what was sown. Whoever has ears, let them hear."*

*Matthew 13:1-9 (NIV)*

Soil matters, and if a seed isn't handled with care in a nutrient-rich environment with adequate water, the tree's survival is limited. Both the soil and environment we grew or are growing up in has helped or is helping to shape our perceptions and perspectives regarding the things of God. The environments we live in could provide the necessary shade to protect us from the scorching sun's heat, provide the nutrients we need to survive, or they can protect us from the animals (ungodly men and women) on the ground looking for prey. All the same, they could do the opposite of what we know and understand, and that is—kill the gifts and talents within us all.

Our environments are used to cultivate the countless beliefs we foster, and they help to build our trust. These atmospheres can help our faith or tear it down. We can either water the seeds (information) within the dirt (our flesh) with the water (Word) needed, or we can leave the dirt dry, not producing the nutrient-rich soil quality needed for the seeds in us to bring forth the cultivation of our full potential.

We can stay in the stage of infancy or we can get to moving towards the mastery of our gifts and talents. Like trees, the environments we are in or leave from affect our productivity and growth from one level to another. We all have places that we thrive in and areas that deplete us. Depletion is not all bad if we set aside more time to be poured into and watered through the Word of God.

My father paraphrases 1 Corinthians 3:6 as *"One-man plants, another waters but God does the increase."* We all have seeds that were planted in us and need watering to grow. Whether planted or watered, both grow tremendously in accordance with what we hear.

*"Seeds of faith are always within us; sometimes it takes a crisis to nourish and encourage their growth."*

*Myles Munroe*

The information from the media we listen to can plant seeds in us, water the seeds that are already in us, or do both. It can give us the right amount of watering to start a business or give us too much information, which would lead to fear and drive us into bankruptcy. The seeds that are filtered through our ears or, better yet, our listening gates have information that could help or hinder our growth, especially if they are watered from the wrong sources.

> *"So then faith cometh by hearing, and hearing by the word of God."*
>
> *Romans 10:17 (KJV)*

So, this means that information that comes from the right source will build our faith. This is the ultimate cultivation piece to the puzzle. Hearing what God said and is saying both allows for what was planted in us and watered by others to grow into what God has purposed it to be. You can read as many books or articles as possible, but the information that you take in will only serve to plant a seed in your heart or to water the seeds that are already there. The Word of God that comes to confirm that information will propel you to your destiny.

On the other hand, we can also choose not to hear the Word of God, and thus add more fuel to conspiracy theories and other ideologies that only serve to tickle our ears, but provide no fuel for our growth or purpose. Howbeit, the ultimate form of increase comes from the Word of God that is heard and applied.

Understanding this provides ways for our wisdom (by faith) to be increased. There is a level of knowledge and understanding that is developed through cultivation and time, and there is a form of wisdom that has to be shaped, molded and pressed until it is ready to be heard. This is the wisdom of faith that must be cultivated through hearing.

*"Knowledge is the gathering of information. Understanding is the interpreting of information (what does it all mean?). Wisdom is the application of knowledge and understanding."*

*A.R. Bernard*

Foundationally, this concept brought forth movements and new eras of thought. It is hidden in both failure and creativity.

We marvel and gaze at people who exemplify faith through their levels of wisdom, knowledge and understanding of the Word of God. Their walks of faith had many pivots and turns, but it was those hardships that grew them into the examples we eventually came to glean from.

The different environments Joseph found himself in molded and shaped him into the man he needed to be. Along with this, the watering provided by the Spirit of God through every relationship built along the way, helped to build Joseph's trust in God in unimaginable ways. And even though it seemed like dirt was being thrown on his name through lies and jealousy, all of the attacks were working for good. They helped to build deep roots into his purpose that would allow him to withstand the weight of helping to rule a nation.

> *"Blessed are those who find wisdom, those who gain understanding, for she is more profitable than silver and yields better returns than gold. She is more precious than rubies; nothing you desire can compare with her. Long life is in her right hand; in her left hand are riches and honor. Her ways are pleasant ways, and all her paths are peace. She is a*

*tree of life to those who take hold of her;*
*those who hold her fast will be blessed."*
                    *Proverbs 3:13-18 (NIV)*

## Chapter 6

# (There are LEVELS and STAGES to This!)

Growing up, I remember the first time I was introduced to comedy through storytelling in the form of a stage play. I can recall being in my grandmother's basement with my family watching a play. We found ourselves on the ground laughing at the things this old lady was saying and doing. We had been introduced to the character "*Madea*" in the play "Diary of a Mad Black Woman." Our family would follow and enjoy many of these plays and movies over the years.

The Madea character was played by the gift that is Tyler Perry. He would become one of the most impactful and prolific modern-day examples of a gift, proving that there are levels to gifting and purpose. Actor, director, screenwriter, producer, author and more, he pioneered the way for many African Americans in the film industry. He allowed us to see that all things are possible for those who believe.

In a conversation with Pastor Joel Osteen at Lakewood Church in Houston, Texas, Tyler gave some amazing points of faith and endurance. He talked about stepping out on faith and producing a play that wasn't having any success. Nevertheless, he still trusted God and believed in his dreams.

While he was working, he'd gotten a call to do a show in South Carolina. According to Mr. Perry, he'd heard a voice that told him to quit his job and go. As he was en route to South Carolina, a hurricane came, canceled his show, thus causing him to become homeless. Howbeit, he still trusted in the dream and vision God had given him.

His mom told him to quit the play and get a job, because she believed that he never would succeed. He stated, *"No matter what, when God has something for you, you have to go for it fully."* He would eventually do the show in South Carolina, but he had also put in the job application his mom told him to submit. He had doubt and was wavering, but God told him to shut up, so he started to listen to the Lord. He looked out the window and saw that the line to get into the play was long. That day was the starting point for his plays being packed out.

From that day to when his plays started to be sold out, something broke in his life. He was going to another level, but also stuck in unforgiveness. This was during the time when he'd produced a play about the abused learning to forgive their abusers. He went on to say, *"Forgiveness is powerful, and it's not for the other person, but for you."* This was a lesson that he'd learned. He'd had a conversation with his father who had been abusive, and he'd said some choice words, but eventually, he'd decided to forgive his father. According to Tyler Perry, the minute he forgave his father was the moment he went from nobody coming to his shows to not having enough seats for the people coming to the shows.

Joel then moved on to ask Tyler about his failures; to this, he said that he didn't have any because he realized that all things were working together for his good. This is another level of faith. When he looked back over all the things in his life that would've looked like failures, he realized that they were teaching and molding moments for him, not failures. If he'd seen his hardship as failures that should not have happened, he wouldn't have been ready for the next moment, nor would he be in the place that he is today. The grace of God brought him to the place he was supposed to be.

Further, he started talking about the creation of Madea and finding out that her humor became an anesthetic for him to be able to deliver serious messages and bring up things that people were dealing with. He would start to talk about sensitive topics that would free people like unforgiveness, overcoming molestation, abuse, and rape.

In a book entitled *"Higher is Waiting"* by Tyler Perry, he discusses these life lessons from his childhood and his career, and so much more. In his book, he explains how to have faith, encouraging his readers to listen to God and take as many steps as needed to reach their goals. Throughout the book, he shared stories of his life that his readers could glean from to learn about the walk of faith and the different levels of faith he went through.

In the final chapter of his book, he uses the anecdote of going on a hike up a mountain with one of his friends. During the climb, he had to stop multiple times to catch his breath. When he would hit clear and leveled ground, he would be able to take big steps and make visible progress, but on difficult inclines, his steps would be very slow and small. He stated, *"The terrain in places was uneven and rough, filled with tangled tree roots, rocks, and ridges.*

*It required plenty of physical effort and focus not to trip."*
He had reached a peak, but soon said:
*"I realized that just because I had touched the top of one peak, it didn't mean I had arrived. This wasn't our destination. There were more valleys to traverse and greater heights to reach. In fact, in order to go higher, we often had to descend first—on and on—down and then up again."*

When he made it to his destination, his friend told him to turn around, and that's when he'd witnessed and was mesmerized by the beauty of the Hawaiian Islands. After managing to catch his breath, he then asked his friend, *"When did we get this high?" To this, she responded, "I don't know. I was in the climb."* Her response made Tyler recall things and events in his life. He said, *"I thought about how difficult it had been for me, chasing down my dream; how hard it was sometimes to believe in where I was going. I thought about the struggle, the pain, the hope—and the moments when I was plagued by doubt. I remembered the times I was working dead-end jobs, moving through my days with my head down, just taking one step at a time—some small ones, some big ones—wanting to give up, wanting to stop and sit for a while, wanting to wallow in my sorrow, nobody believing in me, nobody thinking it would come to pass, and not realizing that every step was taking me closer to this higher place."*

He finalized the chapter saying, *"Sometimes in life, dreams are hard to follow. Just like that climb, you're not aware of how high you're going or if you're even moving. But every step, even when you can't see what's behind you or what's in front of you, brings you closer to your goal. It's in the climb."*

This story and the life of Tyler Perry is all about going from one level of faith to another. Each level has new challenges and tests.

Sometimes, we waver in our faith, and in other times, our faith is small. Growing in faith isn't easy. There are days when we may feel that nothing is working out or times when we think we are not making any strides up the mountains we find ourselves on.

Today, we can see the fruit of Tyler's trust in God and his endurance through the many storms and crises that he'd found himself in. We can see the fruit of his faith through his many plays to him now owning a production studio in Atlanta, Georgia on land that was once a confederate military base. This was a place where the ideologies and beliefs of oppression and slavery ran deep, and now, it is a product of the faith of people like Martin Luther King, Jr. and the countless other men and women who were willing to die for equality.

Learning more about Tyler's faith journey reminds us of Joseph who could have quit, but his faith was built every time he remembered the dream God had given him. Though both Joseph and Tyler may have wanted to quit from time to time, they endured, and their faith grew at each juncture.

In 2008, when I was waiting for the courts to make a decision about my life, the person whose faith level I was amazed by was my father. He didn't seem worried about anything; instead, he'd exemplified a level of faith that I did not understand until now.

Let's dive into some of the levels of faith found in the Bible and the building blocks that we may encounter in life that will allow us to have great and strong faith. There exists different types/stages of faith in the Bible. These types or stages show us the levels of our faith and they can reveal the quality and quantity our faith.

No matter where we are on our faith-walk, we can pinpoint what type of faith we have by looking at how we overcome tough seasons. We can go from having strong faith in one situation to demonstrating little faith in other areas.

If there is a quality of faith, there is a source that determines it and must be known. And if there is a quantity or size of faith, there is an object of faith that determines it. The more we get to know God and grow in His Word, the stronger our faith becomes.

*"When you lose faith, you can't be confident. You become wavering, questioning, weak and all forces of earth run over you."*

Myles Munroe

In 2017, I was introduced to the concept that there are different levels of faith by my pastor and friend, Bryan Meadows. As I was writing this chapter, he was in the middle of a series about faith once again and discussing the varying levels of faith. This prompted me to dig a little deeper. I realized that there was something in the realm of faith that I must research and write about. There were different times in my life that I have found myself experiencing the many types or stages of faith. He began with the teaching entitled "The Measure of Faith" as the basis to our faith journey.

> *"For I say, through the grace given unto me, to every man that is among you, not*

*to think of himself more highly than he*
*ought to think; but to think soberly,*
*according as God hath dealt to every*
*man the measure of faith."*

*Romans 12:3 (KJV)*

Going further into these levels, we learn that
there is little faith. This is mentioned a few
times in the Bible, but one notable mention is
found in the book of Matthew regarding Peter.

*"But Jesus immediately said to them:*
*'Take courage! It is I. Don't be afraid.'*
*'Lord, if it's you," Peter replied, "tell me*
*to come to you on the water.' 'Come,' he*
*said. Then Peter got down out of the*
*boat, walked on the water and came*
*toward Jesus. But when he saw the*
*wind, he was afraid and, beginning to*
*sink, cried out, 'Lord, save*
*me!' Immediately Jesus reached out his*
*hand and caught him. 'You of little faith,'*
*he said, 'why did you doubt?' And when*
*they climbed into the boat, the wind died*
*down."*

*Matthew 14:27-32 (KJV)*

Through this story, we learn that there is a stage of faith called little faith. This is a faith that struggles at times between believing that God can do what He said He will do, hoping that He'll do it, knowing that He can do it, or simply being unsure of whether or not He is willing to do it.

Now, if there is little faith, there has to be a level called great faith. Peter demonstrates a level of great faith simply by stepping out on water while in the midst of a storm. It isn't until he loses focus on Jesus by regarding the wind that his faith changes in size and becomes little. Losing focus caused him to doubt God. Unlike a moment of great faith, there is a level of great faith. This is seen Matthew 8:5-13 when Jesus encounters a centurion who'd asked for help with his paralyzed servant.

> *"Jesus said to him, 'Shall I come and heal him?' The centurion replied, 'Lord, I do not deserve to have you come under my roof. But just say the word, and my servant will be healed. For I myself am a man under authority, with soldiers under*

> *me. I tell this one, 'Go,' and he goes;*
> *and that one, 'Come,' and he comes. I*
> *say to my servant, 'Do this,' and he*
> *does it.' When Jesus heard this, he was*
> *amazed and said to those following him,*
> *'Truly I tell you, I have not found anyone*
> *in Israel with such great faith.'"*
>
> *Matthew 8:7-10 (NIV)*

The centurion knew and understood that whatever Jesus said would be done, even if He wasn't physically present when the healing took place. The words spoken by the Lord were sufficient enough to accomplish whatever Jesus commanded them to accomplish.

Next, there is weak faith and there is strong faith.

> *"Accept other believers who are weak in*
> *faith, and don't argue with them about*
> *what they think is right or wrong. For*
> *instance, one person believes it's all*
> *right to eat anything. But another*
> *believer with a sensitive conscience will*
> *eat only vegetables. Those who feel*

*free to eat anything must not look down on those who don't. And those who don't eat certain foods must not condemn those who do, for God has accepted them."*

*Romans 14:1-3 (NLT)*

*"Someone weak in faith is always looking for things to be perfect."*

*Bryan Meadows*

In March 2016, I received an offer to go and work at the Center for Disease Control and Prevention in Atlanta, Georgia. Prior to this, I had filled out multiple applications around the United States for pharma companies, contract research organizations and government agencies. I had constantly gotten rejected because I'd lacked the work experience required to fill the roles. For some reason, I kept thinking that I was qualified for the positions, even though they required five years of experience, but regardless of what I thought, no job offers came in. I eventually landed on an interesting job posting for the CDC and I applied. This was another job I didn't believe would call back because of the rejections I'd constantly received.

A few days later, I received a call from the CDC. They wanted me to come in for an interview. I was stunned and excited for the opportunity. It was a three-round interview, and I aced the first two. They loved me and the possibility of working at the CDC was looking good. The last interview was with the director of the group. He was an older Black man around my dad's age. We didn't get the chance to get to the technical parts of the interview because we started talking about life, our experiences and family.

I was hoping that if they hired me, I'd be able to learn from him because his experiences were amazing. I received the call back and was offered the position pending a federal background check. I had forgotten that working for the CDC would require a background check and these news caused my faith to dwindle. I started once again believing that I had no chance because of my past record. In that moment, I had both little faith and weak faith. I looked at my past and doubted that I'd be considered for the job because I needed a clearance. Nevertheless, I was cleared and God proved to me who was really in control. This was another key moment in my life that had been used to build my trust and confidence; it taught me to never doubt what God can do. Like Peter, I'd briefly taken my focus off God and looked back at my storms. But just like Jesus picked Peter up out of the water after he'd lost focus, the Lord stepped forward and did the same for me.

Another type of faith that can be experienced in our walk is wavering faith.

> *"But when you ask him, be sure that your faith is in God alone. Do not waver, for a person with divided loyalty is as unsettled as a wave of the sea that is blown and tossed by the wind. Such people should not expect to receive anything from the Lord. Their loyalty is*

*divided between God and the world, and*
*they are unstable in everything they do."*
*James 1:6-8 (NLT)*

Wavering in your faith is dangerous. Other translations refer to this instability as double-mindedness. This is a level of indecision that will get us in trouble. We must move out of this quickly before it's too late.

Now having unwavering faith means to have faith that is unbreakable; it means to trust God without doubt. This is a place we all strive for, and sometimes fail to maintain when faced with difficult circumstances.

> *"Abraham never wavered in believing*
> *God's promise. In fact, his faith grew*
> *stronger, and in this he brought glory to*
> *God. He was fully convinced that God is*
> *able to do whatever he promises."*
> *Romans 4:20-21(NLT)*

Another well-known type of faith is faith without works.

> *"Suppose a brother or a sister is without
> clothes and daily food. If one of you
> says to them, "Go in peace; keep warm
> and well fed," but does nothing about
> their physical needs, what good is it? In
> the same way, faith by itself, if it is not
> accompanied by action, is dead."*
> *James 2:15-17 (NIV)*

This makes faith an action. Not the quality or
quantity, because if faith is by itself, it is dead
without works. We must do something. So,
faith without works just believes and accepts
the Bible, but with no action to back it, proves
to be nothing but a vapor.

In chapter five, we talked about seeds and
trees. There were both a seed and a tree
species mentioned in the Bible that were used
by Jesus to help us understand faith. It is the
mustard seed and the mulberry tree. Here, the
disciples asked Jesus to show them how to
increase in faith.

> *"So, watch yourselves! If another
> believer sins, rebuke that person; then if*

> *there is repentance, forgive. Even if that*
> *person wrongs you seven times a day*
> *and each time turns again and asks*
> *forgiveness, you must forgive."*
> *The apostles said to the Lord, "Show us*
> *how to increase our faith." The Lord*
> *answered, "If you had faith even as*
> *small as a mustard seed, you could say*
> *to this mulberry tree, 'May you be*
> *uprooted and be planted in the sea,' and*
> *it would obey you!"*
>
> *Luke 17:3-6 (NLT)*

A mustard seed is very small. It is around one to two millimeters in diameter. It is one of the smallest seeds in the world. Mustard seeds are known for their health benefits, having antioxidant and anti-inflammatory properties and being high in both nutrients and minerals. A mulberry tree is also known as the sycamore-fig tree; it can live as long as four hundred or more years and can grow to a massive one-hundred feet tall and seventy feet wide. It has one of the largest and deepest root structures growing at thirty feet in depth or more. In the article *"Sycamore Tree Care: How to Grow a Sycamore Tree"* Jackie Carroll states that *"Sycamore trees grow in almost any soil, but they prefer deep, rich soil that is moist but well-drained."* She also stated, *"A sycamore's spreading roots often infiltrate water and sewer lines and damage sidewalks and paved areas."*

So, a mustard seed's worth of *faith* has the spiritual might to move a *mountain* or to transplant a massive sycamore tree into the middle of the ocean. We understand this not just in a literal sense, but within the context of spirituality.

The example of mustard seed faith as told in the Bible speaks to more than just the quantity or strength of our faith, but to the object of our faith; this is what we've placed our faith in. Small faith, when placed in the hands of the all-powerful and Almighty God, becomes great faith, and it is then that great things can happen. All the strength and power we need come from the object of faith (God Himself), not the quantity or size of faith that we believe is needed, after all, just mustard seed-sized faith will do.

*"Your faith is as Big as the God you have it in. But you must know the God you have your faith in."*
*"The more you get to know him the bigger he truly becomes in your life."*

*Myles Munroe*

## Chapter 7

## (Focused on What?)

In our lives, we find ourselves fixating on the things that matter most to us, and at other times, we fixate on the things that are valueless to us. We wonder why we tend to lose focus or how we can be so easily distracted by everything going on around us. There are numerous self-help and motivational books that aim to help us to sharpen and stabilize our focus.

Some days, we can be making strides, while on the other days, we can be pretty motionless. We make excuses in our attempts to explain why we can't focus enough to get things done. What we have heard or seen causes us to develop fears, and these fears paralyze us; they keep us from striving towards our goals and objectives.

Each night, we can find ourselves reflecting on our day, questioning how we've lost so much time. We become unknowingly addicted to things that turn out to be harmful, rather than beneficial to us.

In this rapidly expanding digital age, new technologies are being developed. Some of them are great motivational tools, but they can also be weapons against our purpose. Let's not talk about the many ads that show up everywhere designed to pull on our attention. We are now being bombarded with advertisements through Facebook, Instagram, and other social media outlets that are being advertised as free. If we click one of the ads, we'll soon find ourselves being lured into buying something that we think we need, only to later discover that it was a waste of time and money. Or we look up at our clocks and suddenly realize that we have been trapped in an endless cycle of scrolling on social media, watching one video clip after the other. This is the result of the networks' amazing artificial intelligent algorithms.

The distractions we face daily can be motivators and activators of ideas, or they can be feeding us information that is meant to tear us apart. Our perceptions and perspectives can shift because of the circumstances and issues we are encountering, along with the information we repeatedly take in. The dreams and visions God gave us no longer become our focus. We can become more focused on what is going on via social media in the lives of others, oblivious to the fact that the enemy is stealing and robbing us of our time and enjoying every moment of it.

In 2020, the Coronavirus pandemic was used to either stabilize our focus or distract us. It may have helped us place more focus on the importance of our families and friendships; then again, it may have raised up fears in us, causing us to only focus on the virus itself and what it could potentially do. Remaining focused during the global storm of COVID-19 was hard; at times, it seemed almost impossible to not turn on the news or look at the alerts going off on our phones about it. The focal point of conversations at that time was the virus and the President of the United States.

The questions that now exist are:

- What is getting our attention?
- What activities are draining us of concentration?
- Are we being attracted to and distracted by things and people that are leading us in the wrong direction?
- Are we focused on the things that truly matter for the development and building of our faith?
- Are we focused on one thing or everything which leads to nothing?

In previous chapters, we talked about the three Hebrew boys, along with Joseph, Peter, and Paul. Each of these stories had different focal points. What they focused on revealed their levels of faith in God at the time. The three Hebrew boys focused on the promises of God, despite the decree of death that had been pronounced regarding them. Joseph faced rejection, the betrayal of his family, a sexual assault accusation by Potiphar's wife and being forgotten in prison. Nevertheless, when he had been called upon to interpret the king's dream, he shifted the focus from himself to God. This showed a level of concentration and revealed his faith in the gift that God had given him. Peter had both strong faith and a large amount of faith; this had allowed him to step out on water and walk. But because he had been distracted by the winds, this moment in his life became an example of little faith. Lastly, there is Paul. His faith and trust in God definitely wavered, howbeit, he did not quit. He'd even found himself in prison still being productive and committed to his assignment for the Kingdom. We must understand that before all of this, he had another focus in his prior life. Paul was the name he went by after his direction, perception and understanding changed. It was through an encounter with Jesus that he became Paul, but before his encounter, he was known as Saul.

Saul was responsible for the imprisonment and death of many followers of Christ.

*"I too was convinced that I ought to do all that was possible to oppose the name of Jesus of Nazareth. And that is just what I did in Jerusalem. On the authority of the chief priests, I put many of the Lord's people in prison, and when they were put to death, I cast my vote against them. Many a time I went from one synagogue to another to have them punished, and I tried to force them to blaspheme. I was so obsessed with persecuting them that I even hunted them down in foreign cities."*

*Acts 26:9-11(NIV)*

Saul was so dedicated to eradicating the teachings of Christ and disposing of His followers that he'd hunted believers down by venturing into cities with varying languages, cultures, and customs just to eradicate them. He was determined to promote his own belief system.

On one of his journeys, he'd gone to Damascus to arrest believers, but something happened to shift his focus. God confronted and blinded him in an encounter unlike any he had ever had. This encounter would eventually shift his focus and call into question the things he once believed and would kill for. This encounter was with Christ. It started with the Lord asking him, "Why are you persecuting me?" It ended with Saul realizing that he was in error and asking the question, "Lord, what do you want me to do?" He was now afraid of God; he no longer ascribed to the ideologies and beliefs he'd once promoted. This is where I believe Proverbs 9:10 comes true in the life of Paul.

> *"The fear of the LORD is the beginning of wisdom: and the knowledge of the holy is understanding"*
>
> *Proverbs 9:10 (NIV)*

Saul would eventually regain his natural sight, and he would also gain spiritual insight, hindsight and foresight. This led to the building of a focus so powerful that Paul is attributed to writing almost half of the New Testament.

We can experience having the wind knock our focus out of balance like Peter, or we can be so blinded by God's glory that our attention is arrested, causing us to change directions like Saul. This means that we have to humble ourselves or be humbled. Saul was blind for three days and didn't drink or eat anything. This is what it means to be humbled. Paul was humbled to the point that his new life as Paul helped to not only shift his perspective, but to change the minds of countless people in every generation that came after Paul.

Many of us have been humbled or are being humbled. We may have not experienced the extent of hardships that Paul faced, but we were humbled to the point that we experienced a shift in our outlooks or belief structures. Others have forgotten about the moments used to humble them, and have not taken those moments serious enough to re-adjust their lenses. This leads us into cycles of defeat, causing us to experience the same storms time and time again with no progress.

What if Paul had never answered the call on his life, or if Peter had never taken a step on water? The answer is simple—we wouldn't have these powerful examples of faith on each end of the spectrum. At the end of the day, this faith journey has everything to do with our focus, and we must decide on what deserves our time and attention.

To stabilize our focus, we must be on guard and understand that there are tactics and strategies the enemy uses to throw us off balance; that's only if we allow him to do this. If the enemy can kill, steal, and destroy our focus, he has done his job of limiting our faith. This causes us to fall short of coming into agreement with God's will for our lives.

> *"Be sober, be vigilant; because your adversary the devil, as a roaring lion, walketh about, seeking whom he may devour:"*
>
> *1 Peter 5:8 (KJV)*

Focus is defined as "a center of activity, attraction or attention; a point of concentration" (Merriam-Webster).

Let's dive into the world of photography and some of the types of technological advancements in this arena that can be used to help us understand focus. Many of us have had a front row seat into these advancements through the cameras attached to our phones. We see new phones coming out yearly with cameras that are designed to quickly capture moments with precision. Every year, these cameras seem to have new features, but this is not the arena we want to explore. These advancements come from the knowledge gained in the world of professional level cameras. These cameras have all types of software, mirrors and features added to them to make what we capture come alive.

With a professional level camera, a photographer can change the lens focus to be more detail-oriented, zooming in or zooming out to capture more of what's in front of him or her. The right or wrong amount of light can determine the capacity of what the camera lens can or can't bring into focus. The speed in which the picture is taken can also reveal what the camera is capable of doing. Some cameras can capture keen details, for example, of a bird flying, while for others, this image would be but a mere blur. This is because the blurry image was captured by a camera that didn't have a great sensor or a camera that had low aperture. Nowadays, we can use the cameras on our phones to capture the same image, and just like a professional camera's shot, we'll take some clear and usable shots; then again, we will occasionally take blurry and unusable pictures.

There are many possible choices for camera lens, all of which will give you a different and distinctive image. What type of focus lens matters? You can use a zoom lens; this is a lens designed to capture far-off images if that's your goal, but if you bring a zoom lens to a children's birthday party, you will discover that the lens will serve little to no use. Every lens has an essential distorting quality that is needed to capture the images on the camera's image sensor. This can be anywhere from professionally capturing images or videos for a documentary or movie to using your phone to take selfies. The quality of the lens matters, and what it is attached to determines what can be seen and unseen.

There are some key areas to explore in how a camera can focus on the details afar off with a specific lens, but zoom out and capture more of that same image using a different lens. Alone, the camera may be able to capture small details or larger areas, but with the correct lens attached and adjustments made, the images can become world class. The areas we will explore are focal length, aperture, shutter speed and depth of field.

The focal length within a camera is the primary characteristic to which lenses are categorized. So, what is this focal length? Focal length is "the distance between the center of a lens or curved mirror and its focus" (Google.com). This focal length is measured in millimeters (mm).

Nikon, well known for their cameras and lenses, stated the following, "Lens focal length tells us the angle of view—how much of the scene will be captured—and the magnification—how large individual elements will be. The longer the focal length, the narrower the angle of view and the higher the magnification. The shorter the focal length, the wider the angle of view and the lower the magnification."

The focal length is important in the lens because a photograph taken with a 100mm lens will have a drastically different look than one taken by a 20mm lens. Next, we have what is known as aperture, shutter speed and the depth of field of a lens, all of which are important. Aperture is "the adjustable lens opening that controls the amount of light allowed into the camera" (Adobe). Shutter speed is "a measurement of the time the shutter is open, shown in seconds or fractions of a second: 1 s, 1/2 s, 1/4 s ... 1/250 s, 1/ 500 s, etc. The faster the shutter speed, the shorter the time the image sensor is exposed to light; the slower the shutter speed, the longer the time the image sensor is exposed to light" (Nikon).

Lastly, we have depth of field, which is "the zone of acceptable sharpness in front of and behind the subject on which the lens is focused" (Nikon). Simplified, this means how sharp or blurry the area behind the object will be.

Now that we have a little understanding of the lens, let's look further into a few of the different lenses that operate on numerous focal lengths for varying purposes. The different types of lenses that we will explore are the standard or normal lens, wide angle, telephoto, zoom, fisheye and micro lens types. These are just a few of the categories.

The standard lens is known to fairly reproduce what humans can see in terms of perspective, and the angle of view. It has a standard focal length (50mm,85mm,100mm). Next, is the wide-angle lens, which allows us to do just what the name says—capture a wider angle of view. This lens has a shorter focal length from 10-42mm and is great for capturing outdoor landscapes and group photos. This lens category is said to be one of the only ways to get the complete setting without having any important element in the photo omitted.

The telephoto lenses can give a narrow field of view with a focal length between 100-800mm. They allow us to capture objects from hundreds of feet away and have longer lenses that are great for capturing wildlife. Next, there are zoom lenses that vary in focal lengths anywhere from 24-300mm. These lenses can be used as wide-angle or telephoto lenses. But there are trade-offs in aperture, meaning they have a limited ability to open and allow light in.

After the telephoto lens, we have the fisheye lens. This lens type captures extremely wide images by just changing straight lines into curves, having a focal length ranging from 7-16mm. Lenses in this category can even *"produce circular or oval images by distorting the perspective and creating a 180-degree image,"* writes Attila Kun in his article entitled "Lens Basics."

Lastly, we have the macro lens with a focal length between 50-200mm. These lenses have razor-sharp focus with the macro distance. This allows for an image to be taken of a butterfly or wasp with sharpness. *"Part of the creativity of the photographer is in selecting the right lens to capture the vision of the world the way she or he sees it or wants to present it,"* Attila Kun stated.

So, it is necessary to understand the different lens types and the knowledge needed for photographers to accomplish their assignments. Similarly, the level of focus determines what is in our path or field of view that can distract, distort, or destroy the visions and dreams we have. For example, just like a camera lens can have a zoom-in and a zoom-out feature, which again is determined by the lens attached to the camera, the same is true for us. We can determine what we focus on versus what we ignore. Our focus will determine what we hear or don't hear and can allow us to hone in on the information needed to help our understanding and to ultimately become the key components for developing our faith.

> *"So then faith cometh by hearing, and hearing by the word of God."*
>
> *Romans 10:17 (KJV)*

So, who and what we allow access to our ear gates and eye gates does matter. What we hear and how we hear can determine our perspectives and our perceptions of the events and people around us. But also note that your vantage point will determine what you can and can't see during storms, tests and problems. Filling in these gaps to capture a better picture is vital.

Our lens, of course, would be the information that we take in and the sources by which we gather this information. The lens that we decide to use to get understanding will directly impact our journeys toward purpose and will determine if we arrive at the correct destination; it will also determine how fast we get there. Are we aiming to use a macro lens in our attempts to capture the beauty of an eagle seated at the top of a tree on the peak of a mountain? If so, our lens is out of focus based on the focal length. We must make the necessary adjustments and use a different lens if we want to get clarity and capture the details of the eagle afar off. This is a problem best suited for a telephoto lens.

In every situation Joseph encountered, he had to use the correct lens in order to capture the vision that God had given him. His perspective of the problems allowed him to focus on those problems and zoom in on the promises of God. There were distortions and distractions that Joseph could have stopped to dwell on, but he kept moving and focusing on God's plans that had been revealed to him in his dreams. We must not stay with the standard or normal lens because they have limitations to how far and how wide we can see. We need the ability to see things afar off. We also need clarity and a broader view of the world. This would allow us to see the beauty in the details of God's message to us and help us to grow from every ordered step, obstacle and arena He places us in. This requires us to focus on what is important to God first and foremost. This is a multi-dimensional focus which isn't just natural, but spiritual. Walking, hearing, and working by faith is the key.

*"If Satan can keep you in the sense realm, he will destroy you, but if you keep him in the faith realm, you'll put him under your feet."*

*Fredrick K.C. Price*

## Chapter 8

# (Not This or That, but This and That)

In chapter seven, we explored focus and learned about the types of lenses that serve and have different purposes. Each lens can capture an image which can be interpreted differently; each lens can provide us with views that may be understood or misunderstood because of the incorrect application of the lens. Now knowing this, we can say that perception and perspective are intertwined and designed to keep us focused through the varying trials and tests that we face.

There are three points of view regarding our lives:

1. The way we view ourselves.
2. The way others view us.
3. The way God views us.

*"What you see as a crisis, God sees as an opportunity for growth. What you see as humiliating, He sees as an occasion for the*

*development of humble leadership. It is all in how you see it. What is your perspective?"*
                                    *Myles Munroe*

But coupling this with the level of understanding that is interpreted in different situations, we get three levels of perception:

1. *The way we perceive the situation or problem.*
2. *The way others perceive the situation or problem.*
3. *The way God wants us to perceive the situations and problems we encounter.*

So, it's both our perceptions and perspectives that keep us focused on the goal. In other words, they must work together. Perception is what is interpreted. It is the understanding or the meaning given regarding a situation, person, or object. Perception is "the ability to see, hear, or become aware of something through the senses" (lexico.com). Perspective, on the other hand, is the point of view. It determines how you view yourself, others, and everything else. Perspective is "a particular

attitude toward or way of regarding something"
(lexico.com).

Some believe that our perspective determines
our perception, but in reality, it is the beliefs
that create perceptions that control our
perspectives. It can come either through a form
of repetition, meaning, something developed
by something we learn, see and do repeatedly.
Or the belief came from the many different
tests and trials in our lives.

Once that belief system has been formed and
is focused on, it is then used to extract the
details from our circumstances and create
perceptions using those details. For example, I
perceived that I was an impostor at one time in
my life. It wasn't until that belief was broken off
in my mind that my perception changed and
gave me a new perspective, allowing me to
see through the next set of challenges on my
path.

We all have moments when we defiantly
receive new perspectives through hardships,

and we later want others to have those same perspectives as well. Many times, we fail to change their minds because we haven't come to a place of understanding, and we therefore don't know why they may have a different perspective on a matter. They have perceptions and beliefs working behind the scenes. It isn't until we start doing life with them and loving them through it all that we can possibly be used to help shift any erroneous perceptions or beliefs that they may have.

One of the things I love doing is watching documentaries because these types of films are all about perceptions and perspectives. They can be filled with astounding information, but they are also filled with bias that we must shift through to better understand the story.

We can also receive misinformation and get ensnared by conspiracy theories from a documentary, and these can form beliefs that lead to perceptions, thus causing us to form the wrong perspectives. Understanding another person's beliefs and perceptions may come through us learning about what that person watches, has watched, heard or is hearing.

We must know that many of us are attached to our own beliefs and how we perceive things. Therefore we must treat people who have opposing views with grace, love, and respect. Through time and wisdom, if we stay positive and we remain supportive, allowing our lives to be great examples, any opposing perceptions and beliefs will be broken away from them; that is, if their beliefs are erroneous, and vice versa.

The life of King David is a prime example of someone who had perception and perspective shifts to take place in him and in the people around him because of his relationship with God and the keen understanding he'd received through that relationship. Let's look at two examples in David's life: Goliath and Nathans rebuke. In 1 Samuel 17, we learn about the well-known story of David and Goliath. At that point in time, David was still a boy. He was following the orders of his father, Jesse, and

those instructions were to go and deliver food
to his brothers who were out preparing for war.
They were on the scene of a battle between
Israel and the Philistines. David took the food
to his brothers, and while there, he started to
see the fear that other Israelites, including King
Saul, had towards a giant named Goliath.
Goliath represented the Philistine army.

In verses 25-28, David started to listen to the
men who were talking about the giant. They'd
said that any man who could defeat him would
become wealthy and be given the king's
daughter in marriage. Soon David had a
pointed question for the men around him:

> *"Who is this uncircumcised Philistine
> that he should defy the armies of the
> living God?"*
>
> 1 Samuel 17:16 (NIV)

Here, we start to see that David was not afraid
of Goliath, like everyone around him because
he had some experience. His faith had been
molded and shaped through his encounters
with wild animals, but before he opened his

mouth, we read about an encounter he'd had with his oldest brother. His eldest brother heard David speaking to the men in the camp and had gotten angry. This is why he'd said:

> *"Why have you come down here? And with whom did you leave those few sheep in the wilderness? I know how conceited you are and how wicked your heart is; you came down only to watch the battle."*
>
> *1 Samuel 17:28 (NIV)*

This was a small distraction and David shifted the focus from his brother's attempted rebuke by asking him:

> *"What have I done now?" David replied. "I was only asking a question!"*
>
> *1 Samuel 17:29 (NLT)*

He quickly shifted his attention back to the military men, asking them about the reward he'd receive if he killed Goliath. Soon, word had reached King Saul about this boy who had been expressing interest in fighting Goliath.

Saul called for David, and they have a conversation.

> *"Don't worry about this Philistine," David told Saul. "I'll go fight him!" "Don't be ridiculous!" Saul replied. "There's no way you can fight this Philistine and possibly win! You're only a boy, and he's been a man of war since his youth." But David persisted. "I have been taking care of my father's sheep and goats," he said. "When a lion or a bear comes to steal a lamb from the flock, I go after it with a club and rescue the lamb from its mouth. If the animal turns on me, I catch it by the jaw and club it to death. I have done this to both lions and bears, and I'll do it to this pagan Philistine, too, for he has defied the armies of the living God! The Lord who rescued me from the claws of the lion and the bear will rescue me from this Philistine!" Saul finally consented. "All right, go ahead," he said. "And may the Lord be with you!"*
>
> *1 Samuel 17:32-37 (NLT)*

Saul then gave David his sword and armor, but neither of them fit. David then refused to fight in Saul's armor because he wasn't used to it, so he took it off. We then read about David taking what he believed to be appropriate for him to fight with. He picked up five smooth rocks and placed them in his bag with a sling in his hand, and from there, he proceeded towards Goliath.

Goliath threatened and insulted him.

> "David replied to the Philistine, "You come to me with sword, spear, and javelin, but I come to you in the name of the Lord of Heaven's Armies—the God of the armies of Israel, whom you have defied. Today the Lord will conquer you, and I will kill you and cut off your head. And then I will give the dead bodies of your men to the birds and wild animals, and the whole world will know that there is a God in Israel! And everyone assembled here will know that the Lord rescues his people, but not with sword

*and spear. This is the Lord's battle, and
he will give you to us!"*
*1 Samuel 17:45-47 (NLT)*

Goliath and David moved towards one another,
and that's when David reached into his bag for
a stone. He then put that stone in his sling and
threw it with precision and accuracy towards
the giant, delivering a deadly blow to Goliath.
David then took Goliath's sword and used it to
cut off his head.

David's perception and perspective of the
situation had been different from the others
because of the battles God had allowed him to
go through previously. His focus was different
because of his trust in God, not his own ability.
While everyone saw how large the giant was,
David only saw a mere man who had been
crazy enough to defy the living God. David
believed and trusted God to deliver a win to His
people; this influenced the way he perceived
Goliath and the people around him. David
knew that he was going to win the fight
because his focus never shifted from God to

the noise around him. He had been trained to view and interpret situations differently based on his encounters and victories over lions and bears.

Lastly, there is the story of Nathan and David. During this time, David had lost focus and therefore, his perspective and perception did not line up with God's. David had taken another man's wife named Bathsheba and impregnated her while her husband was serving at war. He sent for the man to come home so he would sleep with his wife; this was his attempt to cover up the act that he'd committed, but David's hopes were shattered when Uriah didn't do what he'd wanted him to do.

> *"David was told, 'Uriah did not go home.' So, he asked Uriah, 'Haven't you just come from a military campaign? Why didn't you go home?' Uriah said to David, 'The ark and Israel and Judah are staying in tents, and my commander Joab and my lord's men are camped in the open country. How could I go to my house to eat and drink and make love to*

*my wife? As surely as you live, I will not do such a thing!' Then David said to him, 'Stay here one more day, and tomorrow I will send you back.' So Uriah remained in Jerusalem that day and the next. At David's invitation, he ate and drank with him, and David made him drunk. But in the evening Uriah went out to sleep on his mat among his master's servants; he did not go home."*

*2 Samuel 11:10-13 (NIV)*

So, he did the unthinkable and abused his power.

*"In the morning David wrote a letter to Joab and sent it with Uriah. In it he wrote, "Put Uriah out in front where the fighting is fiercest. Then withdraw from him so he will be struck down and die."*

*2 Samuel 11:14 (NIV)*

After this, David's perception and perspective was now erroneous because he didn't view his act against Uriah as wrong, nor did he understand why God didn't approve of his actions. It wasn't until Nathan confronted him that his mess was revealed.

> *"The Lord sent Nathan to David. When he came to him, he said, 'There were two men in a certain town, one rich and the other poor. The rich man had a very large number of sheep and cattle, but the poor man had nothing except one little ewe lamb he had bought. He raised it, and it grew up with him and his children. It shared his food, drank from his cup and even slept in his arms. It was like a daughter to him.*
> *Now a traveler came to the rich man, but the rich man refrained from taking one of his own sheep or cattle to prepare a meal for the traveler who had come to him. Instead, he took the ewe lamb that belonged to the poor man and prepared it for the one who had come to him.'*
> *David burned with anger against the man and said to Nathan, 'As surely as the Lord lives, the man who did this must die! He must pay for that lamb four*

*times over, because he did such a thing
and had no pity.'*

*Then Nathan said to David, 'You are the
man! This is what the Lord, the God of
Israel, says: 'I anointed you king over
Israel, and I delivered you from the hand
of Saul. I gave your master's house to
you, and your master's wives into your
arms. I gave you all Israel and Judah.
And if all this had been too little, I would
have given you even more. Why did you
despise the word of the Lord by doing
what is evil in his eyes? You struck
down Uriah the Hittite with the sword
and took his wife to be your own. You
killed him with the sword of the
Ammonites. Now, therefore, the sword
will never depart from your house,
because you despised me and took the
wife of Uriah the Hittite to be your own."*

*2 Samuel 12:1-10 (NIV)*

David could clearly see that God was
disappointed. He had forgotten about what
God had done and all He was doing for him. It

is very important for us to learn that how we see ourselves and how we perceive things does matter, but when our perspectives are not in alignment with how God sees us and what He has already spoken about our lives, our perspectives will amount to nothing. Consequently, we will aim at many targets and hit none of them.

Coming into alignment with God's view, purpose and will for our lives will always serve to sharpen our focus and encourage us to seek after understanding. This understanding and knowledge comes from time spent with God, and it guides us through various situations and circumstances. This allows us to create a new perspective that would have been missed if we'd sought it out on our own or through the lens of others.

Perspectives and perceptions change by spending time with God through prayer, studying and hearing His Word. They are also shifted through our relationships with trusted people who God can use to reveal the erroneous thinking patterns we may have. The only thing more powerful than our problems and our circumstances are our perceptions and perspectives regarding those issues. If we continue to ask for, seek, and pursue the wisdom, knowledge and understanding of God, our perspectives and perceptions will shift, and everything in and around us will start to change.

> *"Ask and it will be given to you; seek and you will find; knock and the door will be opened to you."*
>
> *Matthew 7:7 (NIV)*

## Chapter 9

## (Anxious for What?)

*"Do not be anxious about anything, but in everything by prayer and supplication with thanksgiving let your requests be made known to God. And the peace of God, which surpasses all understanding, will guard your hearts and your minds in Christ Jesus. Finally, brothers, whatever is true, whatever is honorable, whatever is just, whatever is pure, whatever is lovely, whatever is commendable, if there is any excellence, if there is anything worthy of praise, think about these things. What you have learned and received and heard and seen in me—practice these things, and the God of peace will be with you."*

*Philippians 4:6-9 (ESV)*

What is anxiety? Is it the same as fear? If I'm anxious, does that mean that I'm stressed?

These are valuable questions to have answers to and understand.

In order to get understanding regarding what it means to be anxious, we must first dive into fear. There is healthy fear and there is unhealthy fear or phobias. Healthy fear is natural; it is the human reaction to danger. Defined by Merriam-Webster as "*an unpleasant often strong emotion caused by anticipation or awareness of danger,*" healthy fear keeps us from jumping off a cliff or provokes us to move out of the way when a car is speeding down the street in our direction.

If in danger or under threat, the body can go into the response known as "*fight or flight*". This place of fear is momentary, and the response itself is uncontrollable. If a friend decides to sneak up on you in the dark, your response to run or punch them is uncontrollable, but short-lived. If a dog runs towards you barking in an attack mode, your natural reaction is to run. This response is just fine and will not last long. Polly Tig, in her article entitled *"What's the Difference between Healthy Fear and Phobia?"* compared the two in this way:

*"Healthy Fear:*

- *Doesn't affect your daily life.*
- *Is caused by real threats.*
- *Lasts only as long you're in danger.*
- *You forget about the fear once the danger is over.*

*Phobic Fear:*

- *Affects your daily life.*
- *Is caused by perceived threats.*
- *Lasts only as long as you're perceiving danger.*
- *You become fixated or obsessed on the danger reoccurring."*

If we talk about fear and anxiety, we must understand what phobias are. Phobia is *"an intense, persistent, irrational fear of a specific object, activity, situation, or person that manifests in physical symptoms such as sweating, trembling, rapid heartbeat, or shortness of breath, and that motivates avoidance behavior"* (Dictonary.com). Medline

Plus defines the word phobia as *"a type of anxiety disorder. It is a strong, irrational fear of something that poses little or no real danger."*

Anxiety falls into the category of unhealthy fear. Anxiety is caused by being anxious. The word anxious is defined as: *"Full of mental distress or uneasiness because of fear of danger or misfortune; greatly worried; apprehensive"* and Anxiety as *"Distress or uneasiness of mind caused by fear of danger or misfortune"* (Dictionary.com).

In an article entitled "*Anxiety vs Fear*", Shahram Heshmat stated:

*"Anxiety doesn't require a triggering stimulus. It is the anticipation of a threat that is feared, and so anxiety can result in becoming chronically vigilant for potential threats. For example, a panic attack involves the interaction of the fear system with inappropriate and maladaptive learning (i.e., false alarm). Panic is marked by sudden feelings of dread and imminent doom, as well as a number of uncomfortable and distressing physical sensations such as racing heart, difficulty breathing, shaking, stomach*

*and muscle tension, and so forth.This ambiguous nature of anxiety makes it difficult to overcome. If we don't know the source of our anxiety, it is difficult to deal with the problem. It is possible to be anxious about things that will almost certainly never affect us."*

Sheryl Ankrom states in *"The Difference Between Fear and Anxiety"* that:
*"Although the focus of the response is different (real vs. imagined danger), fear and anxiety are interrelated. When faced with fear, most people will experience the physical reactions that are described under anxiety. Fear can cause anxiety, and anxiety can cause fear."*

> *"Therefore, I tell you, do not be anxious about your life, what you will eat or what you will drink, nor about your body, what you will put on. Is not life more than food, and the body more than clothing? Look at the birds of the air: they neither sow nor reap nor gather into barns, and yet your heavenly Father feeds them.*

*Are you not of more value than they?*
*And which of you by being anxious can*
*add a single hour to his span of life?*
*And why are you anxious about*
*clothing? Consider the lilies of the field,*
*how they grow: they neither toil nor spin,*
*yet I tell you, even Solomon in all his*
*glory was not arrayed like one of these.*
*But if God so clothes the grass of the*
*field, which today is alive and tomorrow*
*is thrown into the oven, will he not much*
*more clothe you, O you of little faith?*
*Therefore, do not be anxious, saying,*
*'What shall we eat?' or 'What shall we*
*drink?' or 'What shall we wear?' For the*
*Gentiles seek after all these things, and*
*your heavenly Father knows that you*
*need them all. But seek first the*
*kingdom of God and his righteousness,*
*and all these things will be added to*
*you. "Therefore, do not be anxious*
*about tomorrow, for tomorrow will be*
*anxious for itself. Sufficient for the day is*
*its own trouble."*

*Matthew 6:25-34 (ESV)*

If the enemy can cause us to become anxious and fearful, he has done his job to rob us and destroy certain areas of our lives. The cure for fear-based anxiety is found in Matthew 6:33, which reads, *"But seek ye first the kingdom of God, and his righteousness; and all these things shall be added unto you."* Another antidote can be found in Philippians 4:6, which reads, *"In everything by prayer and supplication, with thanksgiving."*

Fear operates in two dimensions. They are:
- Physical/Natural
- Spiritual

We have natural (healthy) fears, and these are normal. Unhealthy fears, on the other hand, are what Paul referred to in 2 Timothy as the "spirit of fear."

> *"God has not given us a spirit of fear, but of power and of love and of sound mind."*
>
> *2 Timothy 1:7 (KJV)*

This is the fear that fights to destroy our faith. Since faith is spiritual, the spirit of fear is what opposes it and tries to creep into the natural through the gateway of what we see or hear. The spirit of fear can get access to our lives through learned behaviors and attitudes, regardless of our age, our imaginations, ignorance (cultural or willful) and doubt. Paul said that God didn't give us the spirit of fear; this means that the source of fear is the enemy. If we allow him access to our hearts, we simultaneously give him access to diminish faith. In this particular scripture, we find Paul writing to his mentee, Timothy, about this fear to be aware of because he needed encouragement. Paul knew that, like many of us, Timothy struggled with timidity and weak faith. This spirit can place a muzzle on our mouths when God is calling for us to speak out, declaring and decreeing His Word. This spirit causes us to fold and give into our struggles and circumstances. It can birth confusion and it aims to steal and kill the visions and dreams that lead us to our purpose.

The Spirit of God wants us to have and operate in power, love, and with a sound mind. This keeps us focused and moving ahead in God's will for our lives in confidence. Fear wants to oppress and place our minds in prison. It wants us to stay in a place of unforgiveness because we are afraid to address the roots of our issues.

*"FOCUS will DETERMINE FAITH and FAITHLESSNESS will DETERMINE FEAR."*
*Tony Evans*

The effects of the spirit of fear, just to name a few include:
- A divided mind that stifles our abilities to think and act
- Indecisiveness
- Enslavement to the feeling of uncertainty
- The halting of spiritual growth

It affects our physical, mental and above all spiritual health. This can cause many of us to look to others for temporary solutions that are outside of the will of God. We shift our focus on the human's finite ability to try and fix whatever it is we're wrestling with, instead of giving those burdens to God and trusting that He has already worked them out.

The fear that has ran wild in the world through COVID-19 isn't based on just the danger of the virus, after all, this fear is a natural response to a very real issue. The information we've received has planted and watered seeds in us that have caused some of us to become anxious and forget who is in control. The spirit of fear is what is tearing us apart and causing people to make up erroneous theories and conspiracies designed to shift the blame for the virus on people groups or individuals. This spirit wants us to gravitate to an ideology or belief system that paralyzes our movements by arresting our minds. Of course, the fundamental objective is to kill, steal and destroy. The spirit of fear wants us to believe that we are doomed, and that darkness is all around us. It seeks to take control of every move and decision that we make. This is evident by turning on the news and witnessing the effects of the virus and listening to so-called experts trying to rationalize it. These experts only place more fuel on the fire.

The spirit of fear causes us to listen to information coming from sources who have no substance or credibility in the realm of the spirit. All the same, the people we allow access to our ear gates can create valueless belief systems that only seem to work against our assignments. If David had listened to the voices of men around him who'd shivered at the sight of Goliath, we would have lost another key example of what it looks like to walk by faith and trust God. We must understand that at the root of anxiousness, worry or anxiety is fear. This directly aligns with what Paul said:

> *"For we wrestle not against flesh and blood, but against principalities, against powers, against the rulers of the darkness of this world, against spiritual wickedness in high places."*
>
> *Ephesians 6:12 (KJV)*

We must address our fears spiritually. We must question our fears and seek to locate the roots of whatever it is that causes us to worry and be anxious. Do our fears stem from what we are hearing from the people closest to us or are they rooted in our home-grown beliefs? Please note that these fears only serve to limit us and keep us from becoming who God called us to be.

It is crucial that we shift our focus from the fears that have paralyzed our society, and we must take these fears to God in prayer. Prayer is the key to freeing us from those fears. The spirit of fear will always flee at the name of Jesus. Focus on God's Word.

*"Resist your fear; fear will never lead to you a positive end. Go for your faith and what you believe."*

*T.D. Jakes*

Wherever fear was allowed to come in your life, seek to get an understanding regarding that particular subject, and be sure to give the matter to God. Once we submit to God the beliefs that have been bothering us for years, producing fears and limiting us, our faith will grow.

Meditate, study, and seek to apply the understanding and knowledge of God's Word.

> *"So do not fear, for I am with you; do not be dismayed, for I am your God. I will strengthen you and help you; I will uphold you with my righteous right hand. "All who rage against you will surely be ashamed and disgraced; those who oppose you will be as nothing and perish. Though you search for your enemies, you will not find them. Those who wage war against you will be as nothing at all. For I am the LORD your God who takes hold of your right hand and says to you, Do not fear; I will help you."*
>
> *Isaiah 41:10-13 (NIV)*

## Chapter 10

## (Substance and Evidence)

Throughout this book, we have aimed to learn about faith from a few angles. We have come to realize that focus is a fundamental key to discovering what it means to walk by faith. Having a biblical understanding of fear and knowing that fear is the opposing factor that can keep us in bondage helps us stay vigilant and aware of every satanic tactic that can be used to ensnare us. In this chapter, we will explore the two terms that will help us get a better understanding of not just what faith is, but also what faith does.

> *"Now faith is the substance of things hoped for, the evidence of things not seen."*
>
> *Hebrews 11:1 (KJV)*

Faith has substance, and this substance is made up of wisdom, knowledge and understanding. It creates a solid foundation that we can stand on. In other words, we are

147

confident of this thing, even though the thing hasn't birthed fruit or manifested in the natural yet. So, what is substance?

Substance is defined as:
1. *(n.) That which underlies all outward manifestations; substratum; the permanent subject or cause of phenomena, whether material or spiritual; that in which properties inhere; that which is real, in distinction from that which is apparent; the abiding part of any existence, in distinction from any accident; that which constitutes anything what it is; real or existing essence.*
2. *(n.) The most important element in any existence; the characteristic and essential components of anything; the main part; essential import; purport.*
3. *(n.) Body; matter; material of which a thing is made; hence, substantiality; solidity; firmness; as, the substance of which a garment is made; some textile fabrics have little substance.*
*(Webster's Revised Unabridged Dictionary)*

To understand the concept of substance, we
need to understand all of the aforementioned
definitions. With this, we can venture to see
that substance is a vital component of our faith.
Substance can be significant or insignificant; it
can be sufficient or insufficient. We can have
little faith at times, but if we have sufficient
substance, we can still produce great results.
On the other hand, we can think we have great
faith, but have insufficient substance to
produce the results that we desire.

What makes the first part of faith in Hebrews
11:1 important to adhere to is the substance in
which it is attached to. Faith is only as
meaningful and powerful as the substance it
relies on. Substance is the truth that we place
our hopes in. The wisdom, knowledge and
understanding that we have or are seeking
after have substance; that is, of course if we've
acquired that information from the Word of
God.

We all have people in our lives who share
information with us about some things, but we

don't believe them or trust the information that they share with us because the substance of what they share with us is tainted or comes from an unreliable source. In other words, we cannot place our confidence in what they have said. They have a few facts from an unreliable source, and they've blended this information with other facts or non-facts that they've acquired from other sources. They do this to sound educated, but what they share is misleading in every way possible.

On the other hand, there are those whose wisdom is pretty substantial, and we are assured that their information is truthful because it comes from someone who has a track record of providing valuable and credible information. This information often derives from their trust and walk with God.

*"Faith deals with things that are real that have not yet penetrated your five senses because you haven't seen it yet. Hope is an expectation about the future. Hope is an expectation of*

*which you are convinced of or convicted about."*

*Tony Evans*

The second vital component to understand is evidence. Faith is not just substance, but it is also evidence of things not seen. So, what now is evidence? When I think of the word evidence, I am reminded of the crime shows or movies I've seen. In order to solve or prove that a crime had been committed, the pieces of evidence needed to align. These are only parts of the puzzle; they are not the whole picture. They only serve to prove that a crime happened or didn't happen the way the investigators suspect.

Evidence is defined as:

📁🖐 *That which tends to prove or disprove something; ground for belief; proof.*

📄🖐 *Something that makes plain or clear, an indication or sign.*

📄🖐 *Law. Data presented to a court or jury in proof of the facts in issue and*

*which may include the testimony of*
*witnesses, records, documents, or*
*objects.*

*(Dictionary.com)*

Evidence can be seen or unseen. Within the realm of faith, it is unseen because God's timing isn't the same as ours. The way we want things to happen isn't necessarily what God has in mind. His ways are not our ways. Yes, if He said that He will do something, whatever He promised to do will come to pass, just not in the way we expect or can see it coming.

David had faith that he could defeat Goliath, but his substance was five stones and a sling. He didn't need Saul's armor or sword, but he utilized the substantive elements that had proved to be enough to get him through past fights. He didn't know what would happen in his next battle, but he had enough proof from his former battles with lions and bears to know that he would defeat Goliath. David didn't know if the first stone would knock Goliath out. He couldn't see how the battle would transpire, but he trusted that it would be won.

It's not until the correct substances come together with hope and the evidence of things unseen that we qualify for a victory. It is the Spirit that produces fruit, and the fruit of the Spirit is evident, meaning, it is an outward expression of faith. This evidence can be seen in the many victories that we get to enjoy, just like it was seen in the victory that David had over Goliath. David had many testimonies of God protecting, keeping, and providing for him, simply because he trusted God. This became the steppingstone to the next level of his life.

Having both substance and evidence allows for us to move forward, not trying to go around the hurdles that get in our way. Instead, we learn to either plow through or climb over them. This presents us with a structure to build upon and allows us to enter the doors of our next levels.

The evidence of what is unseen starts on the inside of us. Seeds and thoughts are unseen to the naked eye, but once the substances come together, we produce the tangible evidence of that in which was once unseen. It started in our spirit man before it ever made its way to the natural.

The things in our lives that are being built started in the spirit before they ever manifested in our lives. Before you accomplish anything, it must first start with a thought or idea, oftentimes planted by the Spirit of God.

Once I started viewing life through the lens of faith, I began to understand that God allowed the pandemic to come and disrupt our lives. He disrupted my reliance on the news for valuable information and He disrupted my reliance on the meaningless things of this world that I was trying to build upon. I was placed back on track to start thinking about and focusing on research and helping fight the inequity and disparities found in this world.

*"Disruption is the mother of innovation."*

*T.D. Jakes*

You can't be innovative until you are disrupted. Life pivots happen in disruption. The disruption of COVID-19 caused the ingenuity and innovation of the first approved MRNA vaccine to fight and prevent serious illness from this virus.

When we start to have enough substance to build evidence, we then start to build credibility and sustainability. This allows us to stay focused on the goal, no matter what obstacles are presented.

I started running track in seventh grade. I had been told in fifth grade by my gym teacher that I wasn't good enough to run, but two years later, two coaches came into my life to restore my faith and to rekindle my desire to run. They helped me to realize that I was good enough to not just run, but also become a hurdler; that is to run and jump. I had the substance and built upon it. When I was in high school, I couldn't see the evidence of one day becoming good enough to get a college scholarship. At that time, I couldn't see that it would provide a foundation for discipline and character that would lead to both an academic and athletic scholarship.

As a hurdler, I learned the importance of building and training areas of my body that other athletes didn't necessarily have to focus on, such as the hips, leg flexibility and all of the core areas. Both my mental and physical health had to be in top notch shape, or the proof of me not being prepared would have remained unseen until the moment I got in the race. Ninety percent of the race is won in the mind, and if you lose focus while in the race, you have already lost.

There will be times when we are praying to see the evidence that God has answered our prayers, but the way we think the answers will come is not necessarily the way that they will come. Our prayers will be answered in ways we never thought or imagined. Keep praying, but let go and let God's perfect will have its way without being anxious and impatient. Just know that our way isn't the best way; Father truly knows best.

From 2017-2020, I had prayed about going back to obtain a PhD to extend my field knowledge and help lead change in research. I'd planned to go back to school, but then came COVID-19. I could have lost hope, but I kept pushing forward and found myself helping advance Alzheimer's research and fight the Coronavirus through response efforts at the CDC. But in 2021, I am seeing the evidence of what I didn't see in 2017-2020, even through the loss of loved ones and other storms I've faced.

I learned my plans to return to school prior to 2021 wasn't in God's timing, but now is the time, and in October of 2021, I will be starting my PhD journey in Biostatistics. If I would have proceeded on to do it myself, I would have missed all the learning and amazing people I was able to build friendships with. I wouldn't have been able to contribute to some of the phenomenal research I've helped contribute to. I probably wouldn't have been able to enjoy the time that I've shared with my son who was born in December of 2019.

You will have evidence, but it will not be seen the way you think. Trust the process and stay focused. The journey isn't going to be easy, and you will have crises to go through, but if you don't waver or lean to your own understanding you, will find peace and success. God's got you, my friend.

Faith exceeds our education and intellect. It is what fills in the gap and provides the confidence we need to not be afraid. Walking by faith is the most powerful thing we can do. Anything else will keep us enslaved and going in circles.

*"Faith is acting like it is so, even when it is not so, in order that it might be so, simply because God said so!"*

*Tony Evans*

*"So be truly glad. There is wonderful joy ahead, even though you must endure many trials for a little while. These trials*

*will show that your faith is genuine. It is being tested as fire tests and purifies gold—though your faith is far more precious than mere gold. So when your faith remains strong through many trials, it will bring you much praise and glory and honor on the day when Jesus Christ is revealed to the whole world. You love him even though you have never seen him. Though you do not see him now, you trust him; and you rejoice with a glorious, inexpressible joy. The reward for trusting him will be the salvation of your souls."*

*1 Peter 1:6-9 (NLT)*

## Chapter 11

## (The Power of Us)

With fear and hatred being seen and heard all around, living by faith is all we can really do. Operating and walking by faith is the key for hope and loving others who have misguided beliefs, perceptions, and perspectives; these are perceptions and perspectives that have been birthed through the lens of fear and ignorance. Faith gets you to the point of caring about what matters most.

What's most important is loving and living in faith, and creating moments and environments that help us all grow in the purpose God has given us. What we encounter or have encountered and experienced through the many circumstances and problems we've endured has wisdom in it. This wisdom, once extracted, is meant to be shared and experienced with others. Our stories of overcoming should be used to encourage the advancement of others, and help others receive salvation and deliverance from the beliefs and ideologies that may have kept them in bondage. We can't do this walk without others. We need others to walk with us on this faith journey. In other words, we need relationships. We grow tremendously by having people around us who God can use to be the vessels for correction and wise counsel that we need. Without relationships, our faith is limited.

Recall in chapter six when the disciples asked Jesus how to increase their faith. Notice that they were asking together in Luke 17:3-6. These men walked with Jesus together and wrote about the journey from their perspectives in the first four books of the New Testament. Through their writings, we can see that these men had their faith challenged and developed with others who walked with them.

Getting through times of crisis by faith takes having amazing relationships. No one can get through a crisis alone. Our relationships can determine if we will conquer or crumble during hard times.

*"As iron sharpens iron, so a friend sharpens a friend."*

*Proverbs 27:17 (NLT)*

In crisis moments, God will send us friends to strengthen, encourage and support us. There are multiple examples of the importance of relationship in the Bible. David had Jonathan (see 1 Samuel 23:16), Timothy had Paul (see Acts 16:1-5); Paul had Titus (see 2 Corinthians 7:5-6); and Jesus had Peter, James and John (see Matthew 26:36-39) during moments of hardship and testing.

*"For where two or three gather in my name, there am I with them."*

*Matthew 18:20 (NIV)*

God uses the relationships that we have to keep us focused and to cultivate our faith. It can be a family member, friend, mentor, or someone God sends us in a particular season who becomes a friend. I've been blessed to have experienced family, friends, and mentors as the some of the most important support systems in my life. They have given me the hope and encouragement that I've needed to get through my storms.

*"Friends offer more than company; they help us carry out our calling."*

*Dharius Daniels*

Our human relationships are vital, but above all in importance and potency is our relationship with Jesus. This relationship keeps us humble, confident, meek (not weak) and knowing that we are more than conquerors. Growing this relationship through prayer, fasting, thankfulness and obedience will take us to places we've never imagined and to a place of focused living by faith. God does the increasing, but relationships do the planting and watering in our lives.

Let us pray:
*Father, thank you for the person reading this book. Our prayer is that you have been glorified through this writing. To those who are reading or listening to this work, we ask that their faith has grown and their understanding*

*on this becomes foundational to a relationship with you.*

*If there be any crisis, problems, or circumstances that we are experiencing, let your Word be placed in front of those issues and spoken to declare authority, dominion, and power. Give us the faith to know that this too shall pass and help us to trust that you are in control.*

*We declare and decree that every other voice and opposing system to your Word is silenced, and that the peace of God that surpasses all understanding will be our portion in every area of our lives.*

*Let this book plant or water seeds for you to increase them in focus, stature, love, and purpose for your Kingdom's work being done here on Earth. In the precious and matchless name of your Son, Jesus, the Christ.*

*Amen!*